# NOTES ON KURDISH DIALECTS

*The Shadi branch of Kurmanji*
*Sulamania*
*(Southern Turkish Kurdistan)*

A Southern Kurdish Folksong
in Kermanshahi Dialect

# NOTES ON KURDHISH DIALECTS

*The Shadi branch of Kurmanji*
*Sulamania*
*(Southern Turkish Kurdistan)*

A Southern Kurdish Folksong
in Kermanshahi Dialect


**E. S. SOANE**



GYAN

*Published by*

Gyan Publishing House
5, Ansari Road
Daryaganj, New Delhi-110002
Phone: 011-47034999, 9811692060
E-mail: books@gyanbooks.com

*Distribution Network*
gyanbooks.com
India, USA, Canada, UK, Australia, France



ISBN : 978-81-212-4479-4 (PB)
First Published, J.R.A.S. London, 1912

2nd Impression 2020

*Printed at:* Gyan Press, Delhi.



**Notes on Kurdish Dialects**
Author: E. S. Soane

# NOTES ON A KURDISH DIALECT, THE SHADI BRANCH OF KERMANJI

By E. B. SOANE

THIS, one of the most northerly of the Kurdish dialects, spoken by a large tribe of Kurds inhabiting the mountains around Erzerum and to the east towards Bayazid, may be reckoned as one of the most important of the Turko-Kurd tongues on account of the regularity of conjugations of its verbs and richness of grammatical form as compared with other Kurdish tongues. With very few differences it may be classed as a companion dialect to that termed by Lerch and others who have studied northern Kurdish dialects, Kermānjī. A very harsh pronunciation is adopted by the Shādī Kurds, which renders their dialect incomprehensible to the southern Kurd. As in the Kermānjī, the influence of the Chaldean (Neö-Syriac) dialects is here and there apparent, and in a few instances Arabic is employed. Turkish, which might be expected to have furnished a proportion of the common words used, has been very sparsely employed. Considered as a whole, and allowing for differences created by corruption of pronunciation, the dialect appears as a well-preserved old Persian tongue. The Shādī Kurds, in common with some other tribes of the south, claim that their dialect is ancient Persian, and have reserved for it the name of Fārisī.

Some note is here advisable upon the term Kermānjī, or Kurmānjī, which has passed among Orientalists hitherto as the name of a dialect spoken around Bayazid and in Turkish Kurdistan generally. While it cannot be stated that this is an incorrect assumption, there is ground for doubt as to the exact accuracy of the term. Kurds generally, even in the south, have a generic term for "villages"—*kermānj*—and use the name *kermānji* to express the sense "villager", "yokel". The Kurds of the north use the word with the signification of villages, or peoples of Kurdish nationality, and assert that the language may be indifferently termed Kurmānjī or Kurdī, different dialects each carrying its own name and differing widely in even fundamental characteristics.

For example, Kurds of the Shādī tribe, which uses a dialect practically the same as the Kermānjī already mentioned (which should properly be termed Hakārī), term themselves Kurmānj, and use the same name to describe the Zāzā, which is very different. For example—

| | go | come | above | below |
|---|---|---|---|---|
| Kermānjī and Shādī | هَرَة | وَرَة | ژُور | ژِير |
| Zāzā . . . | سُوُ | بِيرِ | بان | جِير |

Tradition has it that Kermānjī was originally the name of a tribe of Kurds inhabiting the mountains of Bayazid and Erzerum and consisting of the main branches of Hakārī and Shādī, and that the name has gradually been extended to include the peoples of Bitlis, Van, Diarbekr, etc.

From the comparative tables appended it will be seen that there exists a difference between the Shādī and the Kurmānjī of Aḥmad Khānī, Hakārī, as set forth in that author's works.

It may be here remarked that the Yazidis, about whom considerable mystery is gathered, speak a dialect of Hakārī, but as Yazidis include in their ranks Armenians and Caucasians as well as Kurds, the sect cannot be said to have any distinctive dialect, as has been stated elsewhere.

The Zāzā dialect above noted, spoken by the Kurds of Erzinjān and Diarbekr, displays very wide differences, and would appear to have preserved the speech of another epoch of old Persian than that of the Kermānjī group.

Most notable among the various differences in the pronunciation of modern Persian and Kurdish is the slovenliness of the latter, elision of consonants, softening and disappearance of vowels, and confusion of verb forms. The Kermānjī group, however, has not followed the usage of other Kurdish dialects in these particulars, except in the repugnance to the pronunciation of خ in certain cases; on the contrary, it has hardened Persian و *vāv* into *f*, or retained the original sound; *b* is also hardened to *f* or *p*. Final *t* after *s* has not fallen into disuse as in every other Kurdish tongue, being well and correctly pronounced in such words as *rāst*, *dast*, *bīst*, etc.

*Z* often changes to *zh*; *t* (ت) is sometimes pronounced as Arabic (ط), and when so pronounced will be written in this character here. Following Kurdish usage *m* has changed to *r* in some cases, ex. Persian اُميد appears as اُريش. *R* whenever possible is rolled violently, a feature of all Persian dialects, whether Kurd, Lur, or otherwise. The Arabic sound *aa*, that of the hamza, as in ماءور, is very common. Another sound peculiar to the dialect is that of *eu*, as in the French word *beurre*. Preceding a long vowel *h* often appears, as in *bhā* for Persian *bād*, and *dheu* for Persian *dī*.

In the following pages the letter ڕ represents the sound *r*, and to express that of *w* the sign ڤ has been adopted.

## THE SUBSTANTIVE

In common with all Kurdish dialects except Kermanshāhī and Jāfī, Shādī forms its plural regularly in آن *-ān*, and most often without the addition of *k* to the noun as in other dialects. Examples—

| | | | | | | |
|---|---|---|---|---|---|---|
| Singular. | جيڤ | تن | آش | كشت | آف | مير |
| Plural. | جيڤان | تنان | آشيان | كشتان | آفان | ميران |

The alternative plurals permissible in Shādī among these six nouns would be جیفکان, آشکان, and میرکان, the other three nouns not permitting the formation in *k*.

In all southern dialects this affixial *k* may be joined to any noun, and even to parts of the verb, but Shādī has reserved for it a more precise use, i.e. its employment only with nouns admitting of a diminutive sense, as—

From خیز *khīz*, "a girl;" خیزکی *khīzakī*.

From در *dur*, "a lie," no diminutive can be formed, though admissible in southern Kurdish.

کر *kar*, "an ass," admits کرکی *karakī*.

چاف *chāf*, "an eye," admits no diminutive, though doing so in southern dialects.

مال *māl*, "a house," admits مالکی *mālakī*.

These nouns, then, carry the double plurals:—

From خیز, خیزکان and خیزان; from کر, کرکان and کران; from مال, مالان and مالکان.

### Case Endings.

#### 1. دا *dā*.

This is very common in Kurdish, occurring as a genitive and objective (more particularly when the noun is the object of a preposition).

Ex. وان له مالدا ایشه بکنه vān li māl*dā* īsha bikina, "let them work at home," where مال is governed by له.

Ex. از بازاردا دیخازم ترم az bāzārdā dīkhāzm tirrim, "I want to go to the bazar," where بازار is governed by له understood.

#### 2. را *rā*.

Alone among Kurdish dialects the Kermānjī group has preserved this objective ending, but has limited its use to pronouns, as مرا, ترا, ورا, مارا, هونرا, وانرا, *marā*, *tarā*, *varā*, *mārā*, *hūnrā*, *vānrā*. The most frequent use is after a preposition, as in the very common phrase ژبومرا, the equivalent of the Persian از برای من.

Ex. فاتحان ژ مرا بخونن, fāteḥān zhe marā bukhūnin, "that they may pray for me" (from the عروض of Ahmadi Khānī Hakārī).

3. آ *ā*.

This is very little used, and its use appears to be originally parallel to that of ها in Persian, that is, as a plural suffix, but it occurs sometimes in an objective sense also, as وان فکردکن ولاتا خراو بکن, vān fukir dakan vilātā kharāv bikin, where the parallel Persian phrase would read آنها فکر میکنند ولایت راخراب بکنند. Plurals with this suffix have a broader signification than the plural in ان, signifying "all", "every", as is seen from the two plurals of کرمانج Kurmānj, کرمانجان Kurmānjān, and کرمانجا Kurmānjā, the first signifying the tribes Shādī and Hakārī and the second Kurds as a race.

In syntax the noun appears in the same position as in Persian and other Kurdish dialects. Example—

Shādī: تو یک مانگاکی به بازاری دو صد پنجه چار غروشان به ژیر مده, tu yek *māngākī* ba *bāsārī* dū sad pinja chār *ghurūshān* ba zhīr mada.

Persian: تو یک ماده گاورا ببر بازار دویست و پنجاه و چهار غروش کمتر نده, tu yak *māda gāvrā* bibar *bāzār* divīst u panjāh u chahār *ghurūsh* kamtar nadih.

It will be noticed that the Shādī shows a much greater precision in the use of the plural termination than does modern Persian, which prefers the use of the singular form for the plural of all objects not human, and in the case of such nouns even forbids the use of a plural termination except to express a certain sense, that of a large but indefinite number, while Shādī insists upon the correct use of the plural inflexion.

The following table shows, as specimens, a number of nouns, and where the Persian is nearer than other Kurdish dialects it is quoted for comparison. The sign K. signifies Kurdish dialects generally, and for comparison some ten dialects are brought into use, which it is not necessary to enumerate. When the Kermānjī (Hakārī) differs from the Shādī it is quoted, but not otherwise.

| Shādī. | Pron. | Other Language or Dialect. | English. | Remarks. |
|---|---|---|---|---|
| باخ | bākh | K. باخ , P. باغ | a garden | |
| بهاو | bhāv | K. ڤا وا با , P. باد | wind | Kji. با |
| بادام | bādām | K. باآم بایم , P. بادام | an almond | Kji. باوام |
| برف | barf | P. برف , K. بفر ڤور ڤفر etc. | snow | |
| چلو | chlū | K. کلا | a leaf | Kji. کلا |
| دری | darī | K. در , P. در | a door | |
| در | dar | K. دشت در , O.P. در | desert, outside | |
| رند | rind | North. K. رنه , P. رنه (able, wily) | good | Kji. خاص رنه |
| قیش | qīsh | P. قاش | a tear, rent | |
| زارو | zārū | K. ژاورا زاورو | a child | Kji. زاوری |
| هری | hurī | O.P. خوری, K. هری خوری | wool | Kji. هرِی |
| میش | mīsh | P. پشه , K. میشی | a gnat | |
| هرژور | harzhivar | O.P. نردبان , K. نردڤان | stairs, a ladder | Kji. نردوان |
| کاغت | kāghat | P. کاغذ | paper | Kji. کاغذ |
| کرسی | kursī | South P. and Ar. کرسی | a chair | |
| دیوار | dīvār | P. دیوار , K. دیڤار | a wall | |
| وی | vī | P. ریش, K. ریش | a beard | |
| دوان | divān | P. دندان , K. دڤان دنان ددان | teeth | Kji. دنان |
| زمان | zamān | P. زبان , K. زڤان | tongue | Kji. زبان |
| دف | daf | P. دبان , K. دَڤ دم | mouth | Kji. دَو |
| لیف | līf | P. لب , K. لیڤ لیچ etc. | a lip | Kji. لیڤ |

| SHĀDĪ. | PRON. | OTHER LANGUAGE OR DIALECT. | ENGLISH. | REMARKS. |
|---|---|---|---|---|
| بری | birī | P. ابرو , K. نوچو بانچو | eyebrows | Kji. برد |
| تیوژ | tüzh | P. تیز , K. تیژ | sharp | Kji. تیژ |
| کیول | kül | P. کند , K. کول کل | blunt | Kji. کول |
| جی | jī | P. جو , K. جیه جه جی | barley | Kji. جِه |
| جیف | jīf | Vulg. P. جیف | a pocket | Kji. جیو |
| نکا | nikā | P. اینگاه | now | |
| گا | gā | P. گاو , K. کا کاف | an ox | Kji. گاف |
| مانگا | māngā | P. ماده گاو , K. مانگا | a cow | |
| پر | pirr | K. فره فر , O.P. فرا | a lot | |
| هندک | handik | P. اندک | a little | |
| مرشک | mirshk | P. مرغ , K. مامر | a fowl | |
| خاو | khāv | P. خواب , K. خاف | sleep | Kji. خاف |
| خفالک | khwālik | P. خواهر , K. خزا خفاشک | sister | Kji. خایشک |
| رفن | rwan | P. روغن , K. رفن | clarified butter | |
| زو | zū | P. زود , K. زو | early | |
| شیلم | shailam | P. شلغم , K. شلم شیلم | a turnip | |
| ترپ | tirp | P. تربیزه , K. ترپ | a radish | |
| کرژنک | kirzhink | O.P. کژدم , K. کلژدم | a scorpion | |
| ایسوت | īsūt | Chaldean Īsaūta | pepper | |
| جیپت | jipt | O.P. چپت | crooked | Kji. جوت |
| قچکه | quchka | P. کچک , K. بچوک | small | Kji. بچوک |
| پسنک | pisink | Vulg. P. پشی , K. پشی پسی | a cat | Kji. پسک |
| جهی | jhī | P. جدا , K. جیه | separate | Kji. جیا |
| آش | āsh | O.P. آس , K. آش | a mill | |
| ماسی | māsī | P. ماهی , K. ماسی | fish | Kji. ماسی |
| نیویه | nīvīa | P. نیم , K. نیمه | a half | Kji. نیمه |
| گشت | qisht | K. کشت | all | |
| برا | barā | K. برار برا | a brother | |

| Shādī. | Pron. | Other Language or Dialect. | English. | Remark |
|---|---|---|---|---|
| خیز | khīz | T. قز | daughter | Kji. کچ |
| شال | shāl | P. شال | a turban | Kji. ساش |
| گاور | gaavir | | the arm | Kji. بال |
| کر | kar | P. خر , K. هر کر | an ass | |
| خالی | khālī | P. خاک , K. خالی | dust | |
| برف | barf | P. برف , K. ڤور وور | snow | Kji. برو |
| تاف طاف | taf, taf | O.P. تاب , K. تاڤ تاو | the sun | Kji. تاو |
| آر | ār | O.P. آذر آگر , K. آئر آگر | fire | Kji. آگر |
| گرمک | garmik | P. گرمی | warmth | Kji. گرمی |
| سار | sār | P. سرد , K. سار | cold | Kji. سار |
| آف | āf | P. آب , K. اڤ او | water | Kji. آو |
| ژنی | zhinī | P. زانو , K. اژنو زانیو | knee | Kji. زنی |
| چاف | chāf | P. چشم , K. چاڤ | eyes | Kji. چاو |
| ناف | nāf | K. ناڤ | inside | Kji. ناو |
| جگر | jigar | P. جگر | liver | |
| گرجی | gurjī | O.P. گُردُه , K. گرچی | kidneys | |
| دنگ | dang | P. بانگ , K. دنگ | noise | |
| ناو | nāv | P. نام , K. ناڤ | name | Kji. ناڤ |
| هورمیش | haurmish | P. ابرشم , K. اورمش | silk | Kji. میش |
| پیرژن | pīrzhin | P. بیرزن | an old woman | |
| سور | sūr | P. سُرخ , K. سور | red | |
| هشینه | hashīna | | blue | |
| مزار | mazār | O.P. مزار | a grave | Kji. گور |
| سیف | sīf | P. سیب , K. سیف سیو | an apple | Kji. سیو |
| تژی | tizhī | P. سیر , K. تیر | full | Kji. تیر |
| دژمن | dizhmin | P. دشمن , K. دژمن | enmity | |
| ری | rī | P. راه , K. ری | a road | Kji. رَی |
| طال | ṭāl | P. تلخ , K. تال | bitter | Kji. تال |

| Shādī. | Pron. | Other Language or Dialect. | English. | Remarks. |
|---|---|---|---|---|
| دست | dast | P. دست , K. دس | the hand | |
| اویش | avīsh | P. امید , K. اویژ | hope | Kji. اوجی |
| هی | hī | K. هیله | an egg | Kji. هیه |
| خوی | khūī | K. خُفَی | salt | |
| سوگ | sūg | P. سنگ , K. برد بر | a stone | Kji. بر |
| رش | rash | North K. رش | black | |
| میر | mīr | P. مرد | a man | |
| دار | dār | P. درخت , K. دار huri دار | a tree | |
| بزن | bizin | P. بُز , K. بزن | a goat | |
| رو | rū | P. روز , K. روژ رو | day | Kji. روژ |
| شاف | shāw | P. شب , K. شف | night | |
| دز | diz | P. دزد , K. دز | a thief | |
| استو | ustū | North K. استو | the neck | |
| کوز | kūz | P. کوزه | a pot | |
| هرم | harm | O.P. امرود , K. ارمو هرمو | a pear | |
| زوی | zevī | P. زمین , K. رڤین | ground | |
| ارد | ard | A. ارض | the earth | |
| ایژنک | īzhiṇk | P. هیزم | wood | |
| دیری | dīrī | P. تگرگ , K. تیر | hail | |
| استریه | istirīa | P. ستاره , K. استار اسّاره | a star | |
| کادینه | kādīna | P. کاهدان | a store-room | |
| تیڤی | tüwī | P. تشنا , K. تینی | thirsty | Kji. تینی |
| بوک | baōk | K. بوک | a bride | |
| زافا | zāfā | P. داماد , K. زاف | a bridegroom | Kji. زاوا |
| دوی | davī | K. دا دالک , P. دایه | a mother | Kji. داو |
| باب | bāb | K. باڤکه باف , P. بابا | a father | |
| اور | avr | P. ابر , K. هڤر اڤر | clouds | Kji. هور |

## PRONOUNS

The personal pronouns "I, thou, he, we, you, they", which are in Persian من *man*, تو *tū*, او *ū*, ما *mā*, شما *shūma*, آنها *ānhā*, are in Shādī as follows:—

1. I, از *az*. This form appears in all the northern dialects of Kurdish, that is Mukri and its sub-dialects and the Hakārī and allied tongues. Its use is strictly limited to a nominative sense, and it cannot appear in the genitive position, as can the pronoun in Persian (اسپ‌من *asp-i-man*, etc.).[1]
2. Thou, ته *ta*. The Hakārī dialect uses تو *tū* as in Persian and other Kurdish dialects.
3. He, she, او *av*. Other Kurdish dialects give for this pronoun *aw*, *awa*, *ā*, *am*, *av*.
4. We, ام *am*. As with the first person singular, this is the nominative form only, the objective and genitive taking other forms. Other dialects present usually *īma*, also *mā* and *māng*.
5. You, هون *hūn*. A very considerable variety of forms appears in other dialects, such as *īwā*, *shmā*, *hūmā*, *tān*, *ūtān*. The Shādī suggests a derivation from the last-quoted, which is old Persian, and is still used in Yezd.
6. They, وان. This is in conformity with nearly all Kurdish dialects, which present *awān* almost without exception, a regular plural of او *av*, *aw*.

The possessive or genitive, which is formed, as in Persian, by the *izāfa* following the object possessed, appears as follows. Taking for the object possessed the word دژمن *dizhmin*, "an enemy," the six forms are as follows:—

1. دژمن من *dizhmin-i-min*. Here the form in universal use appears. The Persian form مرا *marā* is also permissible

[1] Cf. Zend *azim*, 'I.'

in the Kermānjī group, the only one of all the Kurdish tongues recognizing this form.

2. دژمن ته *dizhmin-i-ta*, or ترا دژمن *dizhmin-i-tarā.*
3. دژمن او *dizhmin-i-av*, or ارا دژمن *dizhmin-i-arā*, or اورا دژمن *dizhmin-i-avra.*
4. دژمن مه *dizhmin-i-ma*, or مارا دژمن *dizhmin-i-mārā*, where again the remarkable exactness of the parallel with Persian appears.
5. دژمن هون *dizhmin-i-hūn*, or (very unusual) *dizhmin-i-tārā*, where *-i tā-* is the equivalent of the Persian تان or اتان.
6. دژمن وان *dizhmin-i-vān*, or وانرا دژمن *dizhmin-i-vānrā.*

The objective form is dual, and as follows:—

| | | | | | |
|---|---|---|---|---|---|
| 1. | Me | من | *min* | مرا | *marā* |
| 2. | Thee | ته | *ta* | ترا | *tarā* |
| 3. | Him | او | *av* | اورا | *avrā* |
| 4. | Us | مه | *ma* | مارا | *mārā* |
| 5. | You | هون | *hūn* | تارا | *tārā* |
| 6. | Them | وان | *vān* | وانرا | *vānrā* |

## Pronominal Terminations.

These are in Persian and Kurdish, the possessive terminations affixed to nouns, as دستم *dast-am*, etc., "my hand," and the particles affixed to verbs as میروم *mīravam*, "I go." Shādī, however, does not appear to possess the first variety, and limits its pronominal affixes to use with verbs. The first form appears in the present indicative of verbs, and is placed in comparison with the forms of other dialects.

| Persian. | | Shādī. | | Other Dialects. |
|---|---|---|---|---|
| میخورم | mīkhūram | دخقم | dakhwam | akhwam, khwam |
| میخوری | mīkhūrī | دخقی | dakhw-ī | akhwat, makhwī, khwaīt |
| میخورد | mīkhūrad | دخقه | dakhw-a | akhwa, makhwat, khwat |

| Persian. | | Shādī. | | Other Dialects. |
|---|---|---|---|---|
| میخوریم | mīkhūrīm | دخفن | dakhw-in | akhwīn, makhwīmān, khwaīm |
| میخورید | mīkhūrīd | دخفن | dakhw-in | akhwīn, akhwān, makhwaīn, khwaīn |
| میخورند | mīkhūrand | دخفن | dakhw-an | akhwan, makhwan, khwan |

The terminations of the third person singular and second person plural are similar to the corruption of the same in vulgar Persian, which would render these parts of the verb as میخوره *mīkhūra* and میخورین *mīkhūrīn* (infinitive of verb, خوردن). The third person plural also presents a parallel, which drops the final *d*.

The demonstrative pronouns are او, "that," and و *va*, "this," with regular plurals اوان and وان, which may be compared with other Kurdish dialects using او, اوه, اڤه for "that" and ای, یه, وی for "this".

The pronouns که and چه, "who" and "what", also "which", and the interrogative sense of the same words have exactly the same use as in Persian.

There remain the reflexive pronouns in Persian: خودم "myself", خودت "thyself", خودش "himself", خودمان "ourselves", خودتان "yourselves", خودشان "themselves", formed from the word خود *khwud* (silent و), "self."

The Shādī uses as its root the Kurdish form with what is possibly the old Persian pronunciation, i.e. with و pronounced, but the final *d* is lost — خفه *khwa*. It forms the various persons as follows: خومه *khwama*, تخفه *takhwa*, اوخفه *avkhwa*, خفما *khwamā*, خفتان *khwatān*, وانخفه *vānkhwā*, the pronominal part thus appearing as a prefix in some and an affix in other words.

These are the usual forms, but there exists another set, also very generally used: خفام *khwām*, خفای *khwāī*, خفا *khwā*, امخفا *amkhwā*, هونخفای *hūnkhwāī*, and خفایان *khwāīān*.

## THE ADJECTIVE

Properly speaking, neither Kurdish nor Persian possesses the adjective, as the noun is equally both substantive and adjective, admitting degrees of comparison. Colloquial Persian has practically ceased the employment of the superlative degree, using to express it a phrase تر . . . ازهمه, "than all . . . er," and Kurdish shows the same peculiarity. Persian forms its comparative in *tar* and Kurdish in *tir*, and the use is the same in both languages.

### NUMBERS.

| | PERSIAN. | | SHĀDĪ. | OTHER DIALECTS. |
|---|---|---|---|---|
| 1 | یک | yak | yek | |
| 2 | دو | dū | dū | |
| 3 | سه | seh | seh | |
| 4 | چهار | chahār | chār | chār, chwār |
| 5 | پنج | panj | pinj | panj |
| 6 | شش | shish | shash | shash |
| 7 | هفت | haft | haft | haf |
| 8 | هشت | hasht | hasht | hasht |
| 9 | نه | nuh | niyya | nuh, na, ni |
| 10 | ده | dih, dah | dah | dah |
| 11 | یازده | yāzda | dah o yek | yānza |
| 12 | دوازده | davāzda | dah o dū | dwānza |
| 13 | سیزده | sīzda | dah o seh | sīnza |
| 14 | چهارده | chahārdah | dah o chār | chwārda |
| 20 | بیست | bīst | bīst | bīs |
| 40 | چهل | chihil | chal | chil |
| 50 | پنجا | panjā | pinja | panjāh |
| 60 | شصت | shast | shaīst | shist, shis |
| 70 | هفتاد | haftād | hafta | haftā |
| 80 | هشتاد | hashtād | hashta | hashtā |
| 90 | نود | navad | nawt | nawad, nawa |
| 100 | صد | sad | sat | sad |
| 1000 | هزار | hazār | hazār | hazhār |

The ordinal numbers are formed as in Persian by the addition of either م *-um* or ان, as—

| | | PERSIAN. |
|---|---|---|
| First | پیشی | اوّل |
| Second | دوّم | دوّم |
| Third | سیان | سیّم |
| Fourth | چاران | چهارم |
| Fifth | پنجان | پنجم |
| etc. | | |

## THE VERB

As is the rule in modern Persian and Kurdish, Shādī has lost the bulk of what must originally have been a large number of simple verbs, and supplies the deficiency with compounds. For the rest the Shādī verb does not present so many unusual features as many other dialects, and is very regular in its form.

As a general rule the verb forms its infinitive in final *n*, following the rule of Kurdish, which has either dropped or did not possess the full terminations in *-khtan*, *-tan*, *-dan*, etc. Examples—

کوتن *kūtin*, to fall.
هاتن *hātin*, to come.
آوتن *avatan*, to throw.
ڤاردن *wārdan*, to bring.
کنن *kanin*, to laugh.
رّاکفن *rrā kafin*, to sleep.

These infinitives are very little used in conversation, as is the case in all dialects, various parts of the verb being employed to express the desired meaning.

In the formation of the tenses a very fair consistency is noticeable, and the usage of all the northern dialects is followed, i.e. instead of the Persian prefix *mi-* to form the present indicative *da-* is used. These northern dialects are those which have not come in contact with Lurī and its usages, and have retained what is evidently an ancient form, for it exists here and there even among the mutilated verb forms of the Kermanshāhī and Kurdistānī (Sina). The dialects in which it is preserved intact are, in Persia, Mukrī and its sub-dialects, in Turkey, Hakārī and Shādī.

When the infinitive is not fundamentally simple, as in the case of رّاکفن *rrākafin* (prefix *rrā*) and لیخن *laikhan* (prefix *lai-*) the suffix *-da* does not appear.

In the negative *da-* gives place to *nā*.

In one or two cases also, apart from that of verbs with prefixes, the particle *da-* has disappeared and given place to another letter. The first of these verbs is هرّن *harrin*, "to go," where the present indicative becomes ترم *tirrim*, where the initial *t* is apparently the result of *d* and *h* (دهرم) becoming fused into one sound. This verb is very irregular and forms its preterite from the Kurdish verb چون *chūin*, "to go" (see later).

The second verb worthy of remark upon the irregularity of its present indicative is وارن *vārin*, "to bring," which appears as ترم *tirim*, "I bring," the meeting of *d* and *v* in the regular form having apparently produced the same result as in هرّن. This verb also shows an irregularity in the preterite, which is آنم *ānim*, "I brought," evidently the relic of a verb resembling the Persian and Kurdish آوردن, where in the survival of corruption the initial alif has been preferred to the second syllable.

The third verb, هاتن *hātin*, "to come," also appears in the present indicative as تیم *tim*, apparently a parallel result of the junction of *d* and *h*, as in هرّن. This phase of the consonant fusion has its exact parallel in the southern Kurdish dialects, which from the verbs اوردن (آوردن) and هـاتـن form the present indicatives تیارم *tiāram* and تییم *tiaīm* (Kermanshāhī).

Compound tenses are rarely used in Kurdish, which is generally satisfied with present indicative, preterite, past perfect, past imperfect, and conditional in nearly all its dialects. Where, as in the case of Kermanshāhī, which is gradually taking a regular prose form, compound tenses are formed upon the Persian model, they are rendered very obscure by the inexactness of the verb "to be", and the corruption which has rendered nearly all its parts so much alike as to make definiteness very difficult of achievement. For instance, in the verb "to be" (Kermanshāhī) the preterite appears as ***bīm***, "I was," but in the compound tense of ***dāshtan*** and other verbs, "I had had," the form is ***dāshtüm*** in place of ***dashta bīm***, and while the conditional of the same auxiliary is ***būm***, "if I be," in composition with another verb it becomes ***-ütm***, as ***kirdütm***, "[if] I should do."

The following list of present indicatives of Shādī verbs shows the formation:—

Present indicative of verb "to eat", خُفْن.

دخفم *dakhwam*, I eat.
دخفی *dakhwī*, thou eatest.
دخه or دخفه *dakha*, he eats.
دخفن *dakhwin*, we eat.
دخفن *dakhwin*, you eat.
دخفن *dakhwan*, they eat.

The following are the first persons singular, present indicative, of the infinitives quoted:—

| | INFINITIVE. | PRESENT INDICATIVE. |
|---|---|---|
| فاخفن | *fạkhwan*, to drink | دِفَاخُفَم |
| ليخن | *laikhan*, to strike | ليخم |
| نوسان | *navīsān*, to write | رَنُوسِمَ |
| كنن | *kanin*, to laugh | دكنم |

| | Infinitive. | Present Indicative. |
|---|---|---|
| رّاكتن | *rrākatin*, to lie down | رّاكتم |
| دان | *dān*, to give | دِدِم |
| گوتن | *gūtin*, to speak | دِبِم |
| چى كرن | *chī kirrin*, to cut | چى دكم |
| كفتن | *kaftin*, to fall | دكفم |
| دين | *dīn*, to see, find | ددينم and دديم |
| واندا كرن | *vāndā kirrin*, to be concealed | واندا كم |
| بير كرن | *bīr kirrin*, to forget | بير دكم |
| فكريان | *fikirīān*, to look at | دفكرم |
| رأڤن | *raawin*, to run | درأڤم |
| پينگان | *paīnigān*, to be able | پينگام |
| بون | *būn*, to become | دبوم |
| خازن | *khāzin*, to wish | ديخازم |
| پرسن | *pirsin*, to ask | دپرسم |
| گيشتن | *gaishtin*, to arrive | دگيشم |
| قاى كرن | *qāī kirrin*, to build | قاى دكم |
| | etc., etc. | |

The preterite shows its affinity with Persian and other Kurdish dialects by the absence of verbal prefix, but it places the pronominal particle before instead of after the root in some cases, and permits apparently the observance of either position of pronominal particle. Example: دان *dān*, to give.

| | | | |
|---|---|---|---|
| دام | *dām* | مدا | *madā*, I gave. |
| داى | *dāī* | تدا | *tadā*, thou gavest. |
| دا | *dā* | أودا | *avdā*, he gave. |
| دان | *dān* | امدا | *amdā*, we gave. |
| دان | *dān* | هوندا | *hūndā*, you gave. |
| دان | *dān* | واندا | *vāndā*, they gave. |

There appears to be no rule as to the use of the two forms, euphony apparently deciding the question.

The past perfect (Persian کرده ام *kardar am,* "I have done") is formed as in all Kurdish dialects, i.e. the particle ه (*h*) appears after the pronominal affix instead of being attached to the verb root. Thus, کردن "to do, make".

| | | |
|---|---|---|
| Past perfect, "I have done," | کردمه | kirdima. |
| (etc.) | کردته | kirdita. |
| | کردیه | kirdīa. |
| | کردنه | kirdina. |
| | کردنه | kirdina. |
| | کردنه | kirdina. |

This rule is regular for all verbs.

The past imperfect (Persian میکردم *mīkardam,* "I used to do") shows an inversion of the form appearing in the dialects of Mukrī, Sulaimānia, Jāfī, which introduce دَ before the initial pronominal prefix, as دمکرد *damakird,* "I used to do."

The Shādī, however, produces the form مِدِکر *midikir,* تدکر *tidikir,* اودکر *avdikir,* امدکر *amdikir,* هوندکر *hūndikir,* واندکر *vāndikir.*

The form appearing in Sina and Kermānshāhī also is کریام *kiriām,* کریای *kīriāī,* کریا *kirāā,* کریائن *kīrīaīn,* کریاین *kirīaīn,* کریان *kirīān.*

The conditional follows in its form the Persian, in taking as a prefix to the root *b,* and as an affix the pronominal particle.

Example, from infinitive فکریان "to look at".

| | | |
|---|---|---|
| That I look at | که بفکرم | ki bifkirim. |
| (etc.) | که بفکری | ki bifkirī. |
| | که بفکره | ki bifkira. |
| | که بفکرن | ki bifkirin. |
| | که بفکرن | ki bifkirin. |
| | که بفکرن | ki bifkiran. |

### Auxiliaries.

These are, as in Persian, "to be" and "to become," but as in Kurdish generally they are very incomplete. The parts in general use are quoted below.

To be, بين *bīan.*

| Present Indicative. | | | Preterite. | | |
|---|---|---|---|---|---|
| I am | ام | -am. | I was | بيم | bīm. |
| (etc.) | ى | -ī. | (etc.) | بى | bī. |
| | ه | -a. | | بى | bī. |
| | إن | -in. | | بين | bīn. |
| | إن | -in. | | بين | bīn. |
| | آن | -an. | | بين | bīan. |

| Past Perfect. | | | Conditional. | | |
|---|---|---|---|---|---|
| I have been | بيمه | bīma. | That I be | بوم | būm. |
| (etc.) | بيته | bīta. | (etc.) | بوى | būī. |
| | بيه | bīa. | | بو | bū. |
| | بينه | bīna. | | بون | būn. |
| | بينه | bīna. | | بون | būn. |
| | بينه | bīna. | | بن | bin. |

Imperative, به *ba!*[1] 'be!'

The verb "to become" is even more imperfect, the infinitive is بون, and the parts are formed regularly.

| Present Indicative. | | | Preterite. | | |
|---|---|---|---|---|---|
| I become | دبوم | dabūm. | I became | بوم | būm. |
| (etc.) | دبوى | dabūī. | (etc.) | بى | bi. |
| | دبو | dabū | | بى | bī. |
| | دبون | dabūn. | | بين | bīn. |
| | دبون | dabūn. | | بين | bīn. |
| | دبون | dabūn. | | بين | bīn. |

PAST PERFECT.

| | | |
|---|---|---|
| I have become, | بومه | būma. |
| (etc.) | بونه | būna. |
| | بوه | būa. |
| | بونه | būna. |
| | بونه | būna. |
| | بونه | būna. |

These verbs show almost exact parallels with other Kurdish dialects whose auxiliaries are equally defective.

1. Among all Kurdish dialects Shādī is the only one which employs separate verbs for "to eat" and "to drink". Persian has lost the use of the old verb آشامیدن *āshāmīdan*, "to drink," and Kurdish, like it, uses the verb خُوَاردن (P. خُوَردن) to express both actions. Shādī, however, possesses the verb فخفن *fakhwan*, "to drink," which is obviously constructed from خفن *khwan*, "to eat," support of this assumption appearing in the fact of the imperative being, not بفخفه *bifkhwa*, but فخفه *fakhwa*, following the rule for verbs formed with prefixes, as ليخه *laikha!* from ليخن *laikhan*, and ڕا كف *rrā kaf!* from ڕاكفن.

2. The verb قای كرن *qāī kirrin*, "to construct" (P. قایم كردن), separates the two parts to admit the object, as قـای دخانی دكم *qāī dakhānī dakam*, "I build a house," the object taking a prefixial *d*.

3. The dialect is wanting in some verbs common in Persian and southern Kurdish, notably داشتن *dāshtan*, "to possess," which is expressed by a phrase such as "there is to me" = "I have". Other common verbs missing are (1) پیدا كردن *paidā kardan*, "to find," to express which the verb دین *dīn*, "to see," is used, as in the Mukrī of Persian Kurdistan. (2) یاد گرفتن *yād giriftan*, "to learn." For this is substituted the purely Persian version of the same thing, دست گرفتن *dast giriftan*, which has in colloquial

Persian the meaning of "commencing". The Shādī is دست گرتن *dast girtin*, "to learn." (3) ایستادن, "to stand." This dialect has lost this verb and substituted for it one constructed from the Arabic root سَکَن *sakana*, namely سکّنن *sikkinin*, "to stand."

4. When there is an object to the verb the prefix *da-* may appear in both present indicative and preterite, sometimes separated from the verb, and sometimes repeated, forming an objective inflexion to the noun.

دا چه دوی *dā chi davī?* what sayest thou?
دا چه وا *dā chi wā?* what did he say?

5. The verb "to say" appears to be formed from two roots, and to possess two sets of parts formed from these, but various parts are interchangeable and do not always occur in conjunction with the other parts formed from the root.

The two roots are گو and و, from which appear the infinitives گوتن and وتن *watin*, respectively equivalents of modern Persian and Kurdish.

The parts in use with these infinitives are as follows:—

| | *With* گوتن | *With* وَتن |
|---|---|---|
| Imp. | بگو *bagū.* | ببه *biba* = *biwa* or *biva.* |
| Pres. Ind. | دوم *divim* (from وتن). | دوم *divim* or دبم *dibim.* |
| Preterite | گوتم and مگو | واتم *vatim.* |

There appears to be very little preference in the use of these two verbs, which are repeatedly heard in conversation impartially employed by the same person.

The following is a list of some of the simple and compound verbs:—

بین *bīan*, to be. All Kurdish dialects have the same or very slight variants.

بون *būn*, to become. Ibid.

کوتن ***kartin***, to fall. Kurdish ***kaftin***, ***kaotin***, etc.

هاتن ***hātin***, to come. A purely Kurdish verb appearing in all dialects not possessing a Luri element.

آفتن ***dwutin***, to throw. Persian انداختن.

وارن ***vārin***, to bring. Persian and Kurdish آوردن and هاوردن.

وگرن ***vagirrin***, to turn back. Kurdish هرگردبان , هرکردبان, etc.; Persian برگردیدن.

چی کرن ***chī kirin***, to tie. There is no equivalent in other dialects.

گوتن ***gūtin***, to speak. Persian گفتن; Mukrī کوتن.

خفن ***khwan***, to eat. Persian خوردن ; Kurdish خواردن.

فاخفن ***fakhwan***, to drink.

گرتن ***girtin***, to try, take. Persian گرفتن, "to take;" North Kurdish گرتن, "to try."

کنن ***kanin***, to laugh. Persian خندیدن ; Kurdish خنن and کنن.

ڑا کفن ***rrā kafin***, to sleep. Kurdish خَفتِن ; Old Persian خُفتن.

دان ***dan***, to give. Kurdish دان ; Persian دادن.

بر گرتن ***bar girtin***, to raise. Persian برگرفتن ; Kurdish الگرتن, هرگردن.

فکرن ***fakirin***, to look at. Kurdish نَیرن ; Persian root نگر, نگاد.

گیشتن ***gaishtin***, to arrive. Kurdish the same.

ریژن ***raishin***, to pour. Persian root ریز ; Kurdish رشنان, رشان, ریژان, ریژنان, etc., etc.

آژن ***āshin***, to sow. Persian پاشیدن ; Kurdish واشنان, etc.

کیشنن ***kīshnin***, to pull, draw. Persian کشیدن ; Kurdish کیشن, etc.

ڑآون ***rraarin***, to run. Old Persian رهانیدن ; Kurdish راکردن, etc.

فرتین ***firaitin***, to sell. Kurdish the same; Persian فروختن.

خیونن *khünin*, to read, sing. Kurdish خیونن خَوَانن ; Persian خواندن.

مشان *mashān*, to send.

مرن *mirrin*, to die. Kurdish مرن ; Persian مردن.

پرسن *pirsin*, to ask. Kurdish پرسیان ,پرسین ; Persian پرسیدن.

لرزن *lirzin*, to tremble. Kurdish لرزان , لرزین ; Persian لرزیدن.

ماین *māīn*, to remain. Kurdish منن ; Persian ماندن.

بهیستن *bhīstin*, to tear. Hakārī only, the same.

دین *dīn*, to see, find. North Kurdish دین, "to find."

برّن *birrin*, to cut. Kurdish برین ; Persian بریدن.

ڤکرن *wakirin*, to open. Kurdish واکردن ,کردناوا ; Persian واکردن, بازکردن.

سای کرن *sāī kirrin*, to count. Persian حساب کردن.

بان کرن *bān kirrin*, to call. Persian بانک زدن , بانک کردن.

رونشتن *rūnishtin*, to sit. Old Persian نشتن ; Kurdish نیشتن.

کاٌلین *kaalīn*, to cook. Kurdish کلیان.

شاڤتیان *shawtīān*, to burn. Kurdish سوزنان , سوچیان, etc.

درن *durun*, to sew. Kurdish درزین, دوریان, etc.; Old Persian root درز.

ترسن *tirsin*, to fear. Kurdish ترسین ; Persian ترسیدن.

پیژن *paizhn*, to cook. Persian root پز ; Kurdish root پژ.

پاهتن *pāhtin*, to cook. Apparently formed from the Persian root پخت.

هشتن *hishtin*, to place. Persian هشتن ; North Kurdish هشتن.

ششتن *shshtu*, to wash. Persian شستن ; Kurdish شتن, شوریان, etc.

قت گرتن *qat girtin*, to bite. Kurdish قپ گرتن.

دزین *dizīn*, to steal. Kurdish دزین; Persian دزدیدن.

هلبرین *halbarīn*, to raise. Persian برداشتن.

فرین *farīn*, to fly. Persian پریدن ; Kurdish پرین, etc., etc.

## SPECIMENS OF PROSE

1. آ زِ دِیِف چوم بازاری وچَندُ مِی گِرُتم خازِم بِمِّ درچون هوا پِتِر ساربو چاره ناو شارمام . The syntax is exactly as in Persian, and word for word is in that language من دیروز رفتم بازار وچند گسفند گرفتم خواستم ببرم بیرون چون هوا خیلی سرد بود چاره نبود شهر ماندم .

2. In this specimen the English and Persian appear beneath each word, the English being thus read from right to left.

| | | | | | | | | |
|---|---|---|---|---|---|---|---|---|
| تیم | شنُدُا | روژ | چند | دا | فِرصَن | خُقَدەِ | اگر | Sh. |
| میایم | بعد | روز | چند | داد | فرصت | خدا | اگر | P. |
| I shall come | hence | days | some | gave | chance | God | If | E. |

| | | | | | | |
|---|---|---|---|---|---|---|
| وان | ترم | دڤاره | ژوی شنداتر | تَدَبیوُنَم | و | Sh. |
| بوان | میروم | دوباره | از آن دیرتر | دیدنِ شما | به | P. |
| to Vān | I shall go | again | from them afterwards | see you | to | E. |

| | | | | | | | |
|---|---|---|---|---|---|---|---|
| 3. دبی | رند | هوا | چون | شندا | مانک | دو | Sh. |
| میشود | خوب | هوا | چون | دیگر | ماه | دو | P. |
| becomes | good | the weather | that | hence | months | Two | E. |

| | | | | | |
|---|---|---|---|---|---|
| چون | چیان | هرم | هی | گأیُنَم | Sh. |
| چون | کوه | بروم | است | گانم | P. |
| so that (when) | [to the] mountains | that I go | is | my idea | E. |

| | | | | |
|---|---|---|---|---|
| دست نِگِرم | خُوَم | ایشهُ | وگرم | Sh. |
| دست میگیرم | خودم | کار | برگردم | P. |
| I shall undertake | of myself | work | I return | E. |

The following is the free translation of one of the tales from Sa'adi's *Gulistan* (that of the King and the sea-sick slave) by a Shādī Kurd into his own tongue:—

(1) پادشا بَه غلامِ خُقُادا وگأمیه رونشتنه غلامِ وِی کدِنِز نَدیِ بُوو ندی بُوگای چُرِتبِرِدِ گِری و زاری

(2) كِرِی ولُرزِی جانِ وِی گِرُتُ هَـرجـهِ كِرِن راحَـت نَبُو پـادشـا عَاحزِ بُو و چاره ندی حكیم لِگأمیه

(3) بی گُوُ فرمان دَكِی آز آوُرَا گَرُوَا دَدَم پادشا گُوُ مرحـمـت دَبُـو حكیم فرمان كِر غلام بأونِ ودِترِیِ چنه جاران

(4) غُرغُر كِرو موی سَرِی گِرتی و آلیه گـأمـیه كِشُنَان غـلام وهردو دست پشِت گِأمیه

(5) گِرت چون هات وژور آلیهٔ گأمیه رونشت و قرارگِرت پـادشـا خُواش هات ژِایشی حكیم وگُوچه حكمت هیّ

(6) گوپیشی ناچیانه وترس خندقی وقدرا گأمیه نزانی هـركـس گِلِی دكت لَه رِندی خوا حَقِ آو كه خرابی بوینت كه ,

(7) بزانه چیه

In line 1 the inflexion دا appears after the word خقا, "himself," a parallel to Persian usage.

كأمیه = "a ship". This word is apparently borrowed from the Chaldean *ġaamī* = "a ship".

وی = "of him". Cf. the Persian but not Kurdish use of the same word.

دترِی = "the sea".

چرتری = "shaking" (used here in the place of the phrase محنت كشتی نـیـاز موده in the original).

كرِی وزاری = "weeping and moaning". Mod. Persian كریه وزاری.

Line 2:

لرزی جان وی گرت = "trembling seized upon his body".

لكأمیه = "in the ship". له (*li*) is a very much used Kurdish preposition meaning "in", "from", "of", and "to".

Line 3: گو = "he said".

فرمان دَگی = "thou commandest", in the sense "if thou command".

ازاورا کورا دکم = "I him silent will make".

مرحمت دبو = "it becomes kindness".

بأون = "that they throw".

جاران = "times". The word *jār* is common to the whole Kurdish language.

Line 4: غُرغُر = "gurgling".

آلیه = "on", "to", from the Arabic علی.

Line 5: ژور = "above". This word is common to the northern dialects.

ایشی = "work". This word replaces the Persian کار in nearly all dialects.

هَیّ = "is".

Line 6: پیشی = "first".

ناچیانه وترس خندقی = "he had never gone to the fear of the trench"; i.e. "he had never been in danger of drowning".

گِلی دکت = "makes complaint"; Persian گِلّه.

له رندی خقا = "of his own good".

حق اوکه خرابی بوینت = "his right that he shall see bad".

که بزانه چیه = "that he know what it is" (i.e. good).

The tale in the original Persian is as follows:—

پادشاهی با غلام عجمی نشسته بود غلام هرکزدریا ندیده بود ومحنت کشتی نیآزموده کریه وزاری آغاز کرده ولرزه برانه امش افتاده چنانکه ملاطفت کردند آرام نکرفت ملکرا عیش از او منغض شد و چاره ندانستند حکیمی درآن کشتی بود کفت اکرفرمالی من اورا خاموش کنم پادشاه کفیت غات لطف باشد حکیم فرمودتا

غلام‌را بدریا انداختند باری چند غوطه خورد پس مویش بگرفتند وسوی کشتی آوردند غلام بهر دودست دردنبال کشتی آویخت چون برآمد وگفت وراین چه حکمت بود گفت اول محنت غرق شدن نچشیده بود قدر سلامت کشتی‌را نمیدانست همچنین قدر عافیت کسی داند که بمصیبت گرفتار آید

The following is a literal translation by a Shādī Kurd into his dialect:—

پادشا بَه علام عجمی نمد لناف گامیه رونشته بون غلام هیچ وخت دِنِزا ندی بو وتِرسِ گامیه ندی بو گری و زاری آواز کریه ولرزه ولشه کفتیه هرچه زامَت کِشنان آرام نگرت خُواشی پادشا ژوی بری وچاره ترانن حکمِی و اوگامیه بی گواگر فرمان دَگی ازاورا کروا گم پادشا واغایت دوستی بو حکیم فرمان کرغلاما ورنِزِ باون جند جاران غُرغُر کرژپاش موسری گرتن ولای گامیه آنن غلام وهردو دست پشِت گامیه اویژچون هرهات و گنجی رونشت وقرار کرت پادشا تدبیر حکیم پَسَنی هات وگو و وَه چه حکمت بی گوپیشی ترس خفه بین ندی بو قدر سلامت گامیه نزانی هرچنین قدر عافیت میری بزانت که ومصیبت گِرتیت

As this is exactly parallel with the Persian it may be compared word for word.

---

# NOTES ON A KURDISH DIALECT, SULAIMANIA (SOUTHERN TURKISH KURDISTAN)

By E. B. SOANE

THE short sketch of the Sulaimania dialect of Kurdish here presented is part of the result of a study during residence of several months in and about that town.

The dialect is closely allied to, and its grammatical forms identical with, that of the Mukrī, a widespread tongue probably meriting the title of the main Kurdish language. The dialect used in Sulaimania is spoken with slight variations by the Kurds of Shūān, Qaradāgh Bāna, Sardasht, the Qarachūlān district, and Shahr-i-Zūr (Gul'anbar or Khulmar), whose lands lie around the Sulaimania plain. The language of the bazar is somewhat more developed than that of the district, but as it is only by the addition of technical words imported from the Persian, Turkish, and Arabic, which stand as foreign words, the Kurdish is not affected, nor do words of the native tongue appear to have dropped out to give place to importations. Certain of the Turkish words, which are the same as those adopted by most of the other Kurdish dialects, may be considered almost as a part of the tongue of the district, and have entered from the time of the settlement of Turks in the districts of Kirkuk and Altun Keupru on the plains to the west of this part of the Kurdish mountain system.

Sulaimania is the most southerly point at which the northern and middle — or true type — of Kurdish is spoken. Farther south and east, over the Persian frontier, the correct Kurdish form becomes replaced by the old Persian and semi-Lurish dialects of Aorāmān, Gūrān, Kalhur, and Zangana, which are separated from the Sulaimania and allied Jāf dialects by the River Sīrwān and the considerable mountain systems of Aorāmān and Jūānrū.

Sulaimania, as a centre of the present district, has only existed some 230 years (it was founded by Sulīmān Bābān in A.D. 1677) since its rebuilding upon an ancient site by the founder, who was of the Pishdir district of the Bāban tribe (still found near Erbil), which itself was allied to the Hakkārī race, once the most powerful and authoritative of all Kurdish races, and still a famous tribe and country. By this means the secondary tongue of the Mukrī (above referred to) was extended as far south as Shahr-i-Zūr, a little district previously inhabited by peasants speaking the Aorāmān (or sedentary Gūrān) dialect, that also spoken by the old Ardalān dynasty of Sina in Persian Kurdistan.

The Mukrī language above indicated is spoken in the districts around Sauj Bulāq, and to the east as far as the Turk tribes, north-west to the borders of the Hakkārī Kurds, whose tongue is similar, north to Lake Urumia, and south to Ardalān, the old dialect of which has been driven out by Kurdish, to linger still in Pāva, Palangān, Rīzho, and Aorāmān.

Generally speaking, it is the Sunni tribes of Kurds who use the true Kurdish language, and the Shī'ah tribes whose dialects are those with an admixture of Lur forms in verb, noun, and grammar.

It will therefore be readily understood that the Sulaimanian will comprehend with little difficulty a Kurd of Bitlis or Erzerum or Bayazid, while he is put to some pains to understand the language of the Aorāmānī or Gūrān, who live but a few days' journey away.

The corruptions due to mispronunciation are numerous in Sulaimania, but have been quoted in the following notes in some instances, as they are not without value in affording comparisons with words in Persian, which have developed along the lines of change usual in that language. Some of the bad pronunciation of the townspeople is due, they themselves assert, to the large number of Jews and Chaldeans who were converted to Islam and became Kurds in dress and language after the change, influencing to a small extent the general pronunciation of the place and introducing Arabic and Syriac words.

The local dialect has become fixed, to a certain degree, by the large amount of poetry written by the extraordinarily large number of Kurdish poets who have flourished there. A considerable literature exists, but there is no prose amongst it, and as is usually the case in Kurdistan a large number of poems have been written in Persian and some in the Horām or Aorāmī dialect, formerly the Court language of the old Valis of Ardalān, to which reference has already been made.

The Sulaimanian is often termed Kurmānjī, like that of the Hakkārī and Northern Kurds, and can be counted, as has been indicated, to be a part of the general "Kurmanj"[1] language.

In passing it may be remarked that the dialect quoted by de Morgan in his *Etudes Linguistiques*, tome v, as that of Sulaimania is not that of the immediate district, but of the villages beyond Qara Dāgh, which partakes of the idiom of the Jāf tribe. The Jāfi described in the book is not that of the Jāf tribe at all, but merely that of one of the alienated subsections speaking degraded Kermanshāhī. The true Jāfi is very different from that quoted by him, and is nearer to Sulaimanian.

The pronunciation of the Sulaimanian is remarkably ill-sounding. As in most dialects many fundamental

[1] There is a popular interpretation of this word among the Kurds themselves, who say that it is "Kurdmanj", meaning the "people of Kurds". It is still applied to all peoples of undoubted Kurdish origin.

consonants have entirely disappeared, medial *d* suffering most, giving such examples as

| | | |
|---|---|---|
| *māin,* | for *mādyān,* | a mare. |
| *ayam* | ,, *aidam* | I give. |
| *laiya* | ,, *laida* | strike! |
| *kām* | ,, *kudām* | which. |
| *jū* | ,, *jūd* | a Jew. |
| *baiākh* | ,, *baidāq* | a standard. |

*d* occasionally changes to *l*, as in

*kilīlaka,* for *kilīdaka,* a key

or even to *ñg* (pronounced like *-ng* in English wrong),

| | | |
|---|---|---|
| *tuñg.* | for *tund,* | speedy |
| *ziñga* | ,, *zinda* | alive |
| *paiwañg* | ,, *paiband* | a shackle |

unless the *ñg* be simply the result of losing the final *d* and making the *n* nasal.

*b* has, as in so many Kurdish and Persian dialects, undergone the usual change to *w*, as in

| | | |
|---|---|---|
| *duwāl,* | for *dumbāl,* | a boil. |
| *qurwākh* | ,, *qurbāq* | a frog. |
| *arawa* | ,, *arab* | an Arab. |

In *wafr* (Persian *barf, bafr*) the *w* is not a change, but merely a preservation of *v* in Zend *vafra*; *gh*. which exists in Persian words, often disappears, as in

*dū,* for *dūgh.*
*rūn* ,, *rūghan.*
*dru* ,, *durūgh,* etc.

*st* often softens to *z*, as in

*daz,* for *dast.*
*rāz* ,, *rāst.*

The initial *h* often appears where Persian does not possess it, but it would seem that the Kurdish *h* is not necessarily redundant, but a preservation of the initial *h* in the Zend, to which Kurdish lies much closer than does

Persian. On the other hand, there is a great tendency to add an *h*, as will be seen in the following words:—

| | | | |
|---|---|---|---|
| *hanjuman*, | against Persian | | *anjuman*; Zend *hanjuman*. |
| *hagar* | ,, | ,, | *agar*. |
| *hañgwīn* | ,, | ,, | *angabīn*, cf. English *h* in "honey", the same word. |
| *hātin* | ,, | ,, | *āmadan*.[1] |
| *haor* | ,, | ,, | *abr*. |
| *hushtr* | ,, | ,, | *ushtur*. |
| *hailāna* | ,, | ,, | *lāna*. |

In some dialects, notably that of Sina, there is a tendency to add *h* wherever possible, such recently imported words as *avval* appearing as *hawal*.

*s* has been preserved where Persian has changed to *h*, as in

| | | | |
|---|---|---|---|
| *māsī*, | against Persian | | *māhī*; Zend *masya*. |
| *āsen* | ,, | ,, | *āhan*; Sanskrit *ayas*. |

As in many other dialects, words presenting *kh* in Persian occur with *h* or *k*, as

| | | |
|---|---|---|
| *kar*, | against Persian | *khar*. |
| *hishk* | ,, ,, | *khushk*. |
| *hawir* | ,, Arabic | *khamīr*. |

*g* changes often to *ī*, as

| | | |
|---|---|---|
| *tayar*, | for | *tegarg*. |
| *maish* | ,, | *migas*. |

There are two vowel sounds which are very difficult to indicate adequately on paper; these are the two forms of و met with in such words as—

(1) کولکه, where is represented by a *ū* so narrow as to be almost *ī*, and followed immediately by an almost imperceptible sound of *e* as in *bet*. This diphthong will be represented here by *u̇*.

[1] The common rule of consonant change covers this apparent incongruity. *Amadan* becomes *āwadan* (cf. Bakhtiari, Mamaseni *owaidan*), the *d* hardens. The initial *h* needs no further explanation.

(2) دوست گل, where the *zamma* or *vav* is represented by the same narrow *u*, very short, followed by *o* short, the two forming a diphthong difficult to pronounce. This sound will be represented here by *ụ*.

Apart from these there is the *ü* sound, as of the similarly marked letter in German, and the *w* value of و, which, following Kurdish use I have written ؤ where its value is *w*.

The long *ī* sound, or ی, is, in nearly all cases where the same peculiarity exists in obsolete Persian, pronounced *ai*, as

سیف *saif*, an apple,

شیر *shair*, a lion,

where شیر, meaning "milk", is pronounced *shīr*.

The Mukrī, Sulaimania, and allied dialects are notable for the liquid pronunciation of the letter *l*, exactly as in Russian, which will be indicated here by *ḷ*.

The marked *ñg*, or nasal, has been noted above.

## The Substantive

It is probable that the Sulaimania dialect once possessed all the Kurdish forms of inflexion of the noun, some of which appear in the Mukrī, and nearly all in the Hakkāri and Northern Kurmānj.[1] At present, as in Persian, recourse is had to prepositions to form most of the cases.

The plural is formed, as throughout all pure Kurdish, by the addition of *-ān*,[2] but the termination (originally a diminutive) *-ak* is almost invariably prefixed to the syllable, so that words which in some cases hardly admit of a diminutive sense, adopt them in the colloquial (but not in the written) language, which presents often enough

[1] See my "Notes on a Kurdish Dialect, the Shādī Branch of Kermānjī": JRAS., October, 1909, pp. 898–9.

[2] The final *-al* occurring in Kermanshāhī, Kalhur, and the Persian-adopted *Jāf* is a Lurish ending.

the pure *-ān*. So, in poetry, the plural *pandān*, colloquial *panakān* = "thoughts", "ideas".

On the other hand, a word ending in a vowel takes *-ak-* or *-k-* as a support for the vowels, as in the plural *gaurākān* from *gaurā*, where *gaurāān* would be feeble.

There is no use of the singular form with a plural meaning as is so general in Persian; the plural sense must be expressed by the plural form.

There exists also in Kurdish a definite singular form, which is seen in Persian in the final form *-ī*—

قاطری خریدم *qātirī kharīdam*, I bought one mule.
آدمی آمد *ādamī āmad*, one man came.

The Kurdish has the particle *-ek* which it uses in precisely the same manner—

استرکم کری *aistr-ek-m kirrī*, I bought one mule.
پیاوک هات *pīāwek hāt*, one man came.

not to be confused with—

استرکه ام کری *aistraka-am kirrī*, I bought the mule (dim.).
پیاوکه هات *pīāwaka hāt*, the man (dim.) came.

*Genitive*. This case is formed with the use of *ī* between the thing possessed and the possessor, as

منالی کچم *mināl-ī-kichm*, my daughter's child.
روجی هوین *rujī hāwīn*, a summer's day.

In Sulaimania the particle *-ī-* is sometimes so lengthened as to form the principal sound in the phrase *objective*. There is no case ending or indication of the objective sense.

## *Prepositional Cases*

There still remains in the Sulaimanian dialect the form *-dā*, which is a regular rule in Mukri and Northern dialects, occurring in a noun following a preposition. In Sulaimania it is occasionally heard in the following senses, in the dative and ablative cases :—

هاتم لدەدا *hātm la deh dā* = I came from the village.

رّا کردۆه بو شاردا *rrā kurdawa bō shār-dā* = He has fled to town.

It will be noticed that the word *bo* = "for" is used in place of *ba* = "to", and not infrequently the word *la* = "from" is used in the same sense exactly, a habit still observed by the Kurd when he speaks Persian, it being quite common to hear a Mukrī, Jāf, or Sulaimanian say از کجا میروی, *Az kujā mīravī?* "To where are you going?" translating from his own language *lakū dachī.*

Sulaimania possesses a curious diminutive form in *ūla*, which is rarely encountered in vulgar Persian of Shiraz (in one or two words, as *kūchulū* for *kūcheka*), and in Sina of Persian Kurdistan, as in

*pchukūla* = a small, little one (tiny).
*maishūla* = a little fly, from *maish*, a fly.
*mairūla* = a little ant, from *mūra*.
*kūlaka* = *kū* + *ūla* + *aka*, double diminutive.
*jūlāka* = *jū* + *ūla* + *aka*, double diminutive.

This is very common in Sulaimania.

Below is a comparative list of some of the commoner nouns in use :—[1]

| Sulaimania. | | Remarks. | Meaning. |
|---|---|---|---|
| هور | *haor* | Vulgar Persian *aor*, old form *arra* | clouds |
| با | *bā* | Deletion of final *d* | wind |
| وفر | *wafr* | Zend *vafra* | snow |
| مانگشو | *māngisho* | | moonlight |
| باران | *bārān* | As in Persian | rain |
| تیر | *taīr* | Loss of medial and final *g* | hail |

[1] "Northern" and "Middle" Kurdish are used for Hakkārī, Kermanji (North), and Mukrī, Bilbāsī, Rawandūzī, and Pishdir (Middle).

| Sulaimania. | | Remarks. | Meaning. |
|---|---|---|---|
| ساهل | *sāhul* | As in Mukrī | ice |
| آگر | *āgir* | As in all Kurdish | fire |
| آگردان | *āgirdān* | As in all Kurdish of the north | a stove |
| پلیته | *pḷita* | Inversion of *l* and *t*, cf. Persian *fitīla*; obsolete Persian, however, gives *pilīta*; all apparently from Arabic فتیل | a wick |
| آیم | *āīm* | Deletion of *d* after آ | mankind |
| منال | *minal* | As in Southern Kurdish, *d* has disappeared from *mindāl* | a child |
| کُرّ | *kurr* | As in all Kurdish and in South Persian | a boy |
| کچ | *kich* | North and Middle Kurdish. (?) from Turkish قز | a girl |
| پیاو | *pīāw* | As in all Kurdish and in Lurish | a man |
| ژن | *zhin* | | a woman |
| مرد | *mird* | "The man," Sulaimania and Mukrī use | a husband |
| برا | *brā* | The final syllable *-dar* does not appear in any of the Kurdish tongues in this or other words like *mādar*, *khẉāhar*, *shuhar*, *dukhtar*, etc. | a brother |
| خوشک | *khwaishk* | The root *khwā* as in Persian *khẉāhar* minus *-ar* and with diminutive | a sister |
| باوک | *bāwk* | As in all Kurdish | a father |
| دایک | *dāīk* | The Southern Kurdish gives دالک | |

| Sulaimania. | | Remarks. | Meaning. |
|---|---|---|---|
| زاوا | *zāwā* | Change of *m* to *w* and disappearance of final *d* | a bridegroom |
| ناو | *nāw* | Change of *m* to *w* from نام | a name |
| هتاو | *hatāw* | Corruption of *aftab* with initial *h*. Southern Kurdish shows only the word *khwar* | the sun |
| مانگ | *māng* | As in all old dialects of Persian and in all Kurdish | the moon, a month |
| استاره | *astāra* | Sometimes given an initial *h* | a star |
| بیانی | *baiānī* | Also in Caspian coast dialects | to-morrow morning, the morning |
| سبهینی | *subhainī* | Mukrī also. From Arabic ینی + صبح | the morning |
| نیمرو | *nīmarū* | Mukrī also | noon |
| پاش نیمرو | *pash-i-nimrū* | | early afternoon |
| ایواره | *iwāra* | All Kurdish and obsolete Persian | late afternoon |
| روج | *ruj* | Zend *raocho*, Persian *rūz*. Persian dialect *rūsh* | the day |
| شو | *shaw* | | night |
| دوینه | *dwaīna* | Root دی = yester + ینه | yesterday |
| پیری | *pairī* | Zend *para* | the day before yesterday |
| پار | *pār* | Also obsolete Persian; modern Persian پارسال | last year |
| چور | *chūr* | Also Hakkārī | the face |
| چو | *chaw* | All Kurdish | the eyes |
| ناوچو | *nāūchaw* | ,, | the forehead |
| دان | *dān* | Northern Kurdish also | the teeth |

| Sulaimania. | | Remarks. | Meaning. |
|---|---|---|---|
| دم | *dam* | Northern Kurdish and دَف | the mouth |
| ليڤ | *līw* | The distinction between the two lips appears only in local Sulaimania dialect | the upper lip |
| ليچ | *līch* | | the lower lip |
| نی نوک | *nīnūk* | Persian ناخن, Sanskrit *nakha* | the nails |
| برو | *brū* | Sanskrit *bhru*, other Kurdish بری | the eyebrow |
| برژان | *brzhān* | | the lashes |
| پرچ | *prch* | General Kurdish use; cf. obsolete Persian پرچین, "crooked" | a rainbow, curls |
| آگريجه | *āgirīja* | North and Middle Kurdish | the side locks of a woman |
| قش | *qish* | Also used by Turkomans of the district | tangled hair |
| سمير | *smīr* | Other dialects, *smīl*, *swīl*, etc. | the moustache |
| سنک | *sink* | Also Northern Kurdish | the breast |
| مل | *mil* | Middle and Southern Kurdish. Northern has *ustū*, which is also sometimes used | the neck |
| اموست | *amūst* | Southern dialects use *kilk*, a word signifying "an appendage" | a finger |
| ژنی | *zhnī* | Variation of forms of the same word in all Persian and Kurdish dialects | the knee |
| سقان | *sqān* | Also *isq*; Zend *asta* | a bone |
| سردل | *sardl̥* | | the heart |
| زک | *zik* | As in all Kurdish and Northern Lurish. Persian شکم | the belly |
| لش | *lash* | Persian uses لاش for "a body" or "corpse" | a body, living or dead |

| Sulaimania. | | Remarks. | Meaning. |
|---|---|---|---|
| دار | *dār* | Obsolete Persian, also Sanskrit *dāru*, Zend *dāru* | a tree |
| تری | *tirī* | As in all pure Kurdish | grapes |
| گلا | *glā* | As in all pure Kurdish, except when *g* is hardened to *ch* | a leaf |
| تروزی | *trūzī* | Middle Kurdish | a kind of cucumber, *Cassia fistularis* |
| نیسک | *nīsk* | Middle Kurdish | lentils |
| آلت | *alat* | All Kurdish, except Northern | pepper |
| کالک | *kalak* | All Kurdish. Persian گرمک | a small melon |
| شوتی | *shūtī* | All Northern Kurdish. Southern = شامی | a water-melon |
| هرمی | *harmī* | Obsolete Persian امرود, ارمود | a pear |
| برسیله | *barsiaīlı* | Sulaimania only | unripe grapes |
| لاسک | *lāsik* | Middle Kurdish | a carrot |
| دنک | *dang* | All Kurdish | a noise |
| آسن | *āsen* | Zend *ayanh*, Sanskrit *ayas* | iron |
| زر | *zir* | Obsolete Persian زَر | gold |
| زیۆ | *zīw* | Obsolete Persian سیم | silver |
| پاخر | *pākhir* | Northern and Middle Kurdish use also | copper |
| مز | *miz* | Sulaimania and South Kurdish use | copper |
| خوی | *khūī* | North and Middle Kurdish. Southern = خوٓا | salt |
| برخ | *birkh* | Pehlevi *barak*, Persian *barra* | a lamb |
| بزنک | *bizink* | Other Kurdish, *bizin*, *bizinka* | a goat |
| اسک | *ask* | Preservation of *s* in Sanskrit | a gazelle |

| Sulaimania. | | Remarks. | Meaning. |
|---|---|---|---|
| بیقش | *baiqush* | Turkish *buyaqush* | an owl |
| کلشیر | *kalashir* | All Kurdish, "the lion-headed" | a cock |
| رۆی | *rewī* | " " | a fox |
| هنگ | *hang* | Persian has not preserved the *h*, presenting the obsolete انگ | a bee |
| زردۆاله | *zardwāla* | "The yellow one" | a hornet |
| مرملکه | *marmilka* | Approximately the same in all Kurdish | a lizard |
| دوپشک | *dūpishk* | "Two claws" | a scorpion |
| ۆرن | *waran* | All Kurdish | a ram |
| پز | *pas* | All Kurdish (Middle), Zend *pasa* | a sheep |
| پسنکه | *psinka* | Northern Kurdish | a cat |
| کتکه | *katka* | Sulaimania only | a cat |
| ملوشک | *malushk* | Similar in all Kurdish | a sparrow |
| مرّ | *marr* | Middle Kurdish | a ewe |
| کۆراشک | *kawrāshk* | Middle Kurdish. Southern Kurdish *kāwir* | a sheep |
| ماین | *māīn* | As in all Kurdish, loss of medial *d* | a mare |
| ماسی | *māsī* | Preservation of Zend and Sanskrit *s* | a fish |
| مرشک | *mirishk* | One of many Kurdish variations of Zend root word *maregha* | a fowl |
| میش | *maish* | Loss of medial *g*; cf. Fr. *mouche* | a fly |
| خشی | *khishī* | Similar in all Kurdish | a centipede |
| کرۆیش | *karwīsh* | " " | a hare |
| میرول | *mairūla* | Northern and Middle Kurdish (see text) | an ant |

| Sulaimania. | | Remarks. | Meaning. |
|---|---|---|---|
| الاخ | *ulākh* | Middle Kurdish use. Persian meaning = donkey | any beast of burden |
| ایستر | *aistr* | Obsolete Persian | a mule |
| کرلاخ | *karulākh* | *Kar* + *ulākh* = donkey + beast of burden | an ass |
| ورچ | *wirch* | Cf. other Kurdish, *birs*, *birch*, etc. Persian خرس | a bear |
| چولیکه | *chulaika* | "The inhabitant of wilds" | a sparrow |
| براز | *birāz* | Zend *varaza* | a hog |
| بوق | *būq* | Cf. vulgar Persian غوق (from the sound of the creature) | a frog |
| قالونچه | *qālūncha* | Kurdish also قلچه, etc. | a beetle |
| میشوله | *maishūla* | Diminutive of *maish* | a gnat |
| میش | *maish* | Northern and Middle. Southern gives *maias* | a fly |
| باوش | *baush* | Northern and Middle | the side of the body |
| لوت | *lut* | Northern and Middle | the snout |
| قاچ | *qāch* | Turkoman use | the foot |
| پاژنه | *pāzhna* | Northern Kurdish. Pers. پاشنه | the heel |
| خوری | *khūrī* | All Kurdish, used to name a woollen cloth in Persia about 300 years ago | wool |
| مچیر | *machīr* | All Kurdish | thread |
| رقاله | *raqāla* | Middle Kurdish | the ankle |
| تشی | *tishī* | All Kurdish | a thread spindle |
| مال | *māl* | All Kurdish and Lurish use | a tent or a residence |
| خانو | *khānū* | Northern and Middle only | a house (built) |

| Sulaimania. | | Remarks. | Meaning. |
|---|---|---|---|
| حوش | *haush* | Mid. Kurdish. From Ar. حوش | a court |
| بیر | *bīr* | ,, ,, بئر | a well |
| ژیر | *zhīr* | Middle Kurdish (= that which is underneath) | a room |
| کراس | *kerās* | All Kurdish except Kermanshahi | a shirt |
| دربی | *darpai* | Middle and Mukrī | trousers |
| کوا | *kawā* | All Kurdish. From Arabic قبا | a tunic |
| سلته | *salta* | From Arabic *salta* | a waistcoat |
| گریفان | *girīfān* | All Kurdish; cf. obsolete Persian گریبان, a collar, from "the edge being sewn" | a pocket |
| چایر | *chāir* | Loss of medial *d* | a veil |
| گلوونکه | *giluwanka* | = *gelu* + *band* + *aka* | a necklace |
| ملوونکه | *milwanka* | = *mil* + *band* + *aka* | ,, |
| جلک | *jilik* | All Kurdish; cf. Persian use of *jul* for "horse clothing" | clothing |
| برز | *barz* | All Kurdish. Zend *berez* | a high place |
| برد | *bard* | Northern and Middle; cf. برد in بردستان, a place in South Persia, a stony promontory | a stone |
| کانی | *kānī* | "An excavation," all Kurdish | a well |
| کیو | *kīw* | All Kurdish | a mountain |
| ریگه | *raiga* | ,, | the road |
| چم | *cham* | ,, | a river |
| تم | *tam* | ,, also Persian | mist |
| قور | *qūr* | ,, | mud |
| کولم | *kūlam* | Middle Kurdish. "Blind water," the word *kulaw*, where *w* has not changed to *m*, is also used | a lagoon |

| Sulaimania. | | Remarks. | Meaning |
|---|---|---|---|
| كل | *kal* | All Middle and Northern dialects | a high peak |
| مل | *mil* | ,, ,, | a pass, or neck |
| هاۋین | *hāwīn* | Northern Kurdish also. Old Persian *āf*, Sanskrit *ābhā*, formed by addition of initial *h* + *āv* + *in* (attributive affix) = the sun season | summer |
| گلاۋیژ | *glāwaizh* | | the star Sirius |
| قصه | *qsa* | All Kurdish use; ? for Ar. قصّه | a word |
| درو | *drū* | Disappearance of *gh*. Zend *draugha* | a lie |
| سۆنگ | *swang* | Northern and Middle Kurdish. Obsolete Persian سوگند | an oath |
| زاۋاۋنک | *zāwāwang* | *Zāmād-band* | a wedding |
| بوک | *būk* | Middle and Northern Kurdish | a bride |
| ایش | *aish* | Middle and Northern Kurdish (Southern has ژَن) | an ache |
| شیت | *shīt* | All Kurdish. Old Persian شید | a madman |
| فیر | *fair* | Middle Kurdish | habit |
| شارزا | *shārazā* | "Free of the town," Mukrī and Hakkārī (Middle and Northern) | acquainted with a country |
| خزوره | *khazūra* | Middle Kurdish | a mother-in-law |
| تام | *tām* | From Arabic طعام | taste |
| میشک | *maishik* | Similar change to that in *maish* | the brain |
| ناۋراز | *nawrāz* | Mukrī *nawrās* = "right in the middle" | the centre |
| نۆخا | *nawkhā* | Cf. Persian *naodān* | a spout for water |

| Sulaimania. | | Remarks. | Meaning. |
|---|---|---|---|
| خوی | *khwī* | Similar in all Kurdish | salt |
| ویر | *vīr* | All Kurdish | memory |
| هناس | *hinas* | ,, | breath |
| باورشه | *bārūsha* | Middle and Northern Kurdish "wind-sweeper" | a fan |
| اوٚرشینی | *aōrishaīnī* | Middle and Northern Kurdish "water-pouring" | sprinkling |
| هوٚیر | *hawīr* | Arabic خمیر, change *kh* to *h* and *m* to *w* | dough |
| چیشت | *chaisht* | Persian چاشت very seldom used | food cooked |
| هلکه | *hilka* | Northern Kurdish gives *hek*, Southern *khā* | an egg |
| چرم | *charm* | Old *v* of *charva* changed to *m* (to *b* in Persian) | grease |
| چور | *chaur* | Same as above | a greasy thing |
| قزان | *qazān* | Local use of Turkomans also | a cooking-pot |
| رون | *rūn* | Disappearance of *gh*, all Kurdish | clarified butte |
| کوچک | *kauchik* | Turkish قاشق | a spoon |
| هلوشه | *halūsha* | Initial *h*. Persian آلوچه. Kurdish gives initial *h* in all compounds of آلو ; also cf. Persian هلو, "a peach" | a plum |
| گلچیله | *gulchīla* | Other Kurdish *gurchī*, Lurish *gurdāla* | kidneys |
| دیزه | *dīza* | Obsolete Persian دیزو | earthen pot |
| شوینه | *shwīna* | Middle Kurdish | a large basin |
| بیژنک | *baizhink* | N. Kurdish, from root بیژ, "sift" | a sieve |
| هیلک | *hailak* | Northern Kurdish | a small sieve |

| Sulaimania. | | Remarks. | Meaning. |
|---|---|---|---|
| بتال | *batāl* | From Arabic بطال | emptiness |
| دریک | *darīk* | "What tears" | a thorn |
| قرژاله | *qirzhālā* | Mutilated گرژهره, Persian خرزهره | colocynth |
| درزی | *dirzī* | All Kurdish; root درز, "sew" | a needle |
| کنا | *kunā* | All Kurdish; cf. Persian کون | a hole |
| مزگوت | *mizgut* | Arabic مسجد. Remarkable example of mutilation and consonant change | a mosque |
| نویژ | *nwaizh* | Softening of *m* to *w* | prayer |
| کابرا | *kabrā* | Middle Kurdish | "so-and-so," a fellow |
| برین | *brīn* | Middle Kurdish and Northern, from root بر, "cut" | a wound |
| هرق | *haraq* | Erroneous initial *h*; Arabic عرق | sweat |
| هاجزی | *hajizī* | Erroneous initial *h*; from Arabic عاجز | fatigue |
| ایش | *īsh* | Mid. and North. Turkish ایش | work |
| هشک | *hishk* | Middle and Northern Kurdish; cf. Persian هوش | thought |
| سام | *sām* | All Kurdish and obs. Persian | fear |
| خریک | *kharīk* | Middle and Northern Kurdish | employed, busy |
| گرک | *gerek* | Middle Kurdish, also Turkish | necessary |
| پرت | *prt* | Northern Kurdish | a bridge |
| کلک | *kilk* | Obsolete Persian and modern Southern Kurdish meaning = "a finger". Sulaimania and Mukrī use it with the meaning of | a tail |
| رشواله | *rashwāla* | "The black fellow" | a swift |

| Sulaimania. | | Remarks. | Meaning. |
|---|---|---|---|
| كله | *kulla* | Northern and Middle Kurdish | a locust |
| بازرگان | *bāzargān* | Obsolete Persian | a merchant |
| جانباز | *jānbāz* | ,, | a broker |
| چرچی | *chirchī* | Mid Kurdish and local Turkish | a pedlar |
| دروسی | *draūsī* | Mid. Kurdish, "him at the door" | a neighbour |
| تنشت | *tanisht* | Middle Kurdish | alongside |
| شین | *shīn* | Other Kurdish *hashīn*, obsolete Persian *khashīn* | blue |
| سور | *sur* | All Kurdish | dark red |
| ال | *āl* | Middle and Northern Kurdish and Turkoman | full red |
| رش | *rash* | Middle and Northern Kurdish | black |
| سپی | *spī* | Middle and Northern Kurdish (Southern Kurdish = *charmū*) | white |

## The Verb

The Sulaimanian verb presents features of great interest and is here quoted fully, and a moderately complete list of its verbs is given. These impart to Kurdish generally (for the Sulaimanian are very little different from those of Hakkārī, Kurmānjī (North), and Mukrī) that character which allows it at once to stand as a different language from Persian, and not a corrupt dialect.

Every sense that the Persian can obtain with its verb forms can be expressed by the Kurdish by its own very dissimilar forms, which may be compared by students with those of old Iranian tongues.

The verb "to be" demands first attention, and one is confronted immediately with its similarity to the verb "to become", a feature common to Kurdish and Lurish; cf. Bakhtiari *bīa* = "it has been", *būa* = "it has become", and other examples. The similarity is so great as to at first engender a belief that they are one and the same verb, but examination shows otherwise.[1]

I place the two verbs side by side here, showing only the simplest moods, which are most used.

The infinitives are—

بیین ***bīan***, to be

بون ***būn***, to become

as in all Kurdish dialects.

*Present Indicative*

| "To be" | | | | "To become" | | | |
|---|---|---|---|---|---|---|---|
| AFFIRMATIVE. | | NEGATIVE. | | AFFIRMATIVE. | | NEGATIVE. | |
| ام | *am* | نیم | *nīm* | ابم or دبم | *abim* or *dabim* | نابم | *nābim* |
| ای | *ī* | نیت | *nīt* | ابیت ,, دبوت | *abīt* ,, *dabūt* | نابیت | *nābīt* |
| ه | *ah* | نیه | *nīa* | ابی ,, دبو | *abī* ,, *dabū* | نابی | *nābī* |
| این | *īn* | نین | *nīn* | ابین ,, دبون | *abīn* ,, *dabūn* | نابن | *nābin* |
| این | *īn* | نین | *nīn* | ابین ,, دبون | *abīn* ,, *dabūn* | نابن | *nābin* |
| این | *īn* | نین | *nīan* | ابن ,, دبن | *abin* ,, *dabin* | نابن | *nābin* |

The dual form in the affirmative of "to become" is due to the loss of initial *d* (the sign of the present indicative in Kurdish verbs), which is replaced in the more southerly of the true Kurdish dialects by initial *a*, and in either form provides one of the truest signs of a Kurdish or Lurish tongue, for the latter uses no prefix in this place except the Southern dialects (Bakhtiari, Mamaseni, Kuhgelu. etc.), where an initial *ī* occurs, corrupted from Persian *mī*.

In the negative form of the verb "to become" we have probably *nā* + *bim*, for in dialects using only *da-* in the

[1] See my "Notes on the Shādī Branch of Kermānjī": JRAS., October, 1909.

affirmative it is replaced by *nā* in the negative, such a form as *nādabim* never occurring.

*Preterite*

| "I was," etc. | | | | "I became," etc. | | |
|---|---|---|---|---|---|---|
| بوم or ام بو | *bum* or *am bū* | Negative formed by prefix *nā*. | | بوم | *būm* | Negative formed by prefix *nā*. |
| بوی ,, ات بو | *būī* ,, *at bū* | | | بوی | *būī* | |
| بو ,, ای بو | *bū* ,, *ī bū* | | | بو | *bū* | |
| بون | *būn* | | | بون | *būn* | |
| بون | *būn* | | | بون | *būn* | |
| بون | *būn* | | | بون | *būn* | |

The verb "to be" shows here an irregularity which does not occur in Mukrī, etc., which shows بیم, *bīm*, etc. For note on the formation of preterite with initial pronominal forms, see after.

*Perfect*

"I have been," etc.

| Affirmative. 1 | | 2 | | 3 | | Negative. | |
|---|---|---|---|---|---|---|---|
| بومه | *būma* | بیمه | *bīma* | ام بُوه | *ambūa* | نم بوه | *nambūa* |
| — | — | — | — | ات بُوه | *atbūa* | نت بوه | *natbūa* |
| بوه | *būa* | — | — | بُوه | *būa* | نی بوه | *naibūa* |
| — | — | — | — | امان بُوه | *amān būa* | نمان بوه | *namānbūa* |
| — | — | تان بیه | *tān bīa* | تان بُوه | *tān būa* | نتان بوه | *natānbūa* |
| — | — | ایان بیه | *ayān bīa* | ایان بُوه | *ayān būa* | نیان بوه | *nayānbūa* |

The two verbs here are in such similarity that it is necessary only to indicate that form 3 of "to be" is the regular form for "to become", the negatives being identical.

The imperfect sets, Nos. 1 and 2, are met with in their entirety in other allied dialects.

### *Conditional Form*

(Equivalent of Persian باشم and بشوم)

"To be" "To become"

With *hagar* = "if"

| | | | |
|---|---|---|---|
| هگر بیم | *hagar bīm* | هگر ببم | *hagar bibim* |
| هگر بیت | *hagar bīt* | هگر به بیت | *hagar bi biait*[1] |
| هگر بی | *hagar bī* | هگر ببیه | *hagar babaya* |
| هگر بن | *hagar bin* | هگر ببن | *hagar bibin* |
| هگر بن | *hagar bin* | هگر ببن | *hagar bibin* |
| هگر بن | *hagar bin* | هگر ببن | *hagar bibin* |

### *Imperative*

| "Be!" | | "Become!" | |
|---|---|---|---|
| بی | *bī!* | به | *ba!* |
| بین | *bīn!* | بن | *bin!* |

### *Past Participle*

| | | | |
|---|---|---|---|
| بیه | *bīa* | بوه | *būa* |

### *The Infinitive*

This is formed, as in all Kurdish dialects, by *-n*, *-in*, or *-din*.

In connexion with infinitive terminations it may be noted that most of the Persian verbs ending in *-khtan* have their root ending in *z*, as—

*bākhtan* = *bāz*
*sākhtan* = *sāz*
*āmūkhtan* = *āmūz*, etc.,

and Kurdish has in every case where it uses the same root formed its infinitive from it direct, as—

*sāzin*, from *sāz*,
*bāzin* ,, *bāz*, etc.

[1] There is a form *bibiaitin* which follows Lurish use, and is very occasionally heard in Sulaimania.

## *The Present Indicative*

The regular Kurdish verb forms the present indicative on the model of *da* + √ + pronominal particle, but in the southern forms *ai* or *a* takes the place of *da*[1] (the *d* having been weakened and dropped, as is so common), and a little variation may occur in the pronominal terminations, particularly in the second person singular, where *-it* often takes the place of *ī*, as *aizhit* for *aizhī*. Again, by a coincidence, the same confusion may occur in the 3rd singular, where the Kurdish *ī* = "he" may be replaced by the Persian *-ad* hardened to *-it*. It is therefore possible for—

*aizhī* to mean "thou speakest", or "he speaks",
or *aizhit* ,, ,, ,, ,,

owing to the similarity of form but difference of meaning of the purely Kurdish and the Kurdo-Persian suffixes. This confusion, however, occurs as a rule only in dialects where a proximity to Lurish or Gūrān tongues has led to the interchangeability of form.

In Sulaimania town as a regular thing it may be said that the *ai-* prefix in the present indicative is heard as often as the *da-*, which was formerly universal. A kind of custom has thus sprung up by which certain verbs are constructed with *da-* and others with *ai*, which distinction will be shown in the verb tables.

The following is the present indicative of a regular verb:—

From *kaotn*, "to fall"

| Affirmative. | | Negative. |
|---|---|---|
| اكوم | *akawam* | ناكوم, etc. |
| اكوى | *akawī* | |
| اكوى or اكود | *akawī* or *akawa* | |

[1] This is particularly noticeable in the modern dialect of Sina of Ardalan, Persian Kurdistan.

AFFIRMATIVE.

| | |
|---|---|
| اکۆن | *akawan* |
| اکۆن | *akawan* |
| اکۆن | *akawan* |

From *iḷn*, "to speak"

Both prefixes are equally used.

| | | | |
|---|---|---|---|
| ایلم | *aiḷm* | دلم | *daḷim* |
| ایلی | *aiḷī* | دلی | *daḷī* |
| ایلی or ایله | *aiḷī* or *aiḷa* | دلی or دله | *daḷī* or *dala* |
| ایلن | *aiḷn* | دلین | *daḷain* |
| ایلن | *aiḷn* | دلن | *daḷn* |
| ایلن | *aiḷn* | دلن | *daln* |

Negative = نیلم *naiḷm*, etc., for both forms.

The liquid *ḷ* makes this a very difficult verb to pronounce properly, *ḷn* becoming a peculiar concrete sound.

A very large number of verbs have prefixial words (adverbs, etc.), such as *hal*, *par*, *tai*, *lai*, *dā*, which are so closely connected, and so easily form junctions with another word, as to appear at first sight an integral part of the verb. So closely are they joined that the modifying letter of the verbal tense is lost in many cases, e.g.:

1. *laikhistn* = to strike hard.
2. *laidān* = to pulverize.
3. *feradān* = to cast away.

*Present Indicatives*

| 1. | 2. | 3. |
|---|---|---|
| *laikham.* | *laiam.* | *ferayam.* |
| *laikhī.* | *layī.* | *feraiyī.* |
| *laikha.* | *laia.* | *feraya.* |
| *laikhin.* | *layan.* | *ferayin.* |
| *laikhin.* | *layin.* | *ferayin.* |
| *laikhan.* | *layan.* | *ferayan.* |

### *Preterite*

The Sulaimania tongue follows the proper Kurdish use here. The regular form is (from *kaotn* = "to fall", "I fell", etc.).

| | | | |
|---|---|---|---|
| ام كۋت | *-am kaot* | امان كۋت | *-emān kaot* |
| ات كۋت | *-at kaot* | اتان كۋت | *-itān kaot* |
| ای كۋت | *-ī kaot* | ایان كۋت | *-ayān kaot* |

There is a form which serves all purposes to Lurish and Southern Kurdish, but which is, among the pure Kurdish, only used when the verb itself forms a complete sentence, and in the affirmative only. It is—

| | | | |
|---|---|---|---|
| كۋتم | *kaotm* | كۋتمان or كۋتن | *kaotimān* or *kaotin* |
| كۋتی | *kaotī* | كۋتان ,, كۋتن | *kaottān* ,, *kaotin* |
| كۋت | *kaot* | كۋتیان ,, كۋتن | *kaotayan* ,, *kaotan* |

This is necessary, as the regular form required some letter before the pronominal prefix of the regular form, even if it be only the negative, as *namkaot* = "I fell not", for which it is not permissible to use the Lurish and South Kurdish *nakaotm*, the negative of the alternative form. The use of the alternative is therefore very limited, as any sentence with a word in front of the verb provides the necessary support for the regular form. Example of both uses : *la barzīm kaot* = "I fell a long way", equivalent to *la barzī* + *am kaot*, the pronominal prefix joining itself to the preceding word.

*Kaotm* could only be used if no other words were uttered.

The answer to such a phrase might be : *Chlūnit kaot ?* = "How didst thou fall ?" not *chlūn kaoti ?*

### *Past Imperfect*

This form, in Persian, constructed of *mī* + √ + pronominal affix, in Southern Kurdish √ + *īā* + pronominal affix, occurs but rarely, the preterite or perfect form being usually employed. Occasionally, however, the Southern Kurdish form is heard—

"I used to fall," etc.

| | | | |
|---|---|---|---|
| کۋتیام | *kaotīām* | کۋتیان * | *kaotīāin* |
| کۋتیای * | *kaotīāī* | کۋتیان * | *kaotīāin* |
| کوتیا | *kaotīā* | کۋتیان | *kaotīān* |

* The Kermanshāhī کۋتیایت, کۋتیامن, کۋتیاتن are never used.

*Perfect*

"I have fallen"

This is quite regular, and follows the pure Kurdish usage = pronominal form + √ + *awa*, as follows:—

| Affirmative. | | Negative. |
|---|---|---|
| ام کۋتۋه | *am kaotawa* | نم کۋتۋه |
| ات کۋتۋه | *at kaotawa* | نت کۋتۋه |
| ای کۋتۋه | *ī kaotawa* | نی کۋتۋه |
| امان کۋتۋه | *amān kaotawa* | نمان کۋتۋه |
| اتان کۋتۋه | *atān kaotawa* | نتان کۋتوه |
| ایان کۋتۋه | *ayān kaotawa* | نیان کۋتۋه |

In the case of verbs with a prefixial word with the infinitive as *laikhistu* (see before), the form becomes naturally—

| Affirmative. | | Negative. |
|---|---|---|
| لیم خستۋه | *laim khestawa* | لیم نخستۋه |
| لیت خستۋه | *lait khestawa* | لیت نخستۋه, etc. |
| لی خستۋه | *laī khestawa* | |
| لیمان خستۋه | *laimān khestawa* | |
| لیتان خستۋه | *laitān khestawa* | |
| لیان خستۋه | *layān khestawa* | |

The negative changes position from its place before the pronominal prefix (see simple verb) owing to its place being already occupied

*Perfect Past*

This is seldom used, and has three forms, the first of which is most heard—

| 1 | | 2 | | 3 | |
|---|---|---|---|---|---|
| ام كوتووه | *am kaotūwa* | كوتو بوم | *kaotū būm* | كوتومه | *kaotūma* |
| ات كوتووه | *at kaotūwa* | كوتو بوى | *kaotū būī* | كوتوته | *kaotūta* |
| اى كوتووه | etc. | كوتو بو | *kaotū bū* | كوتووه | *kaotūwa* |
| امان كوتووه | | كوتو بون | *kaotū būn* | كوتونه | *kaotūna* |
| اتان كوتووه | | كوتو بون | *kaotū būn* | كوتونه | *kaotūna* |
| ايان كوتووه | | كوتو بون | *kaotū būn* | كوتونه | *kaotūna* |

The third form is that commonly heard in Sina of Ardalan (Persian Kurdistan) and Kermānshāh, and the first is the purest Kurdish. The compound infinitive verb shows—

| | |
|---|---|
| لےم خستووه | *laim khestūwa* |
| ليت خستووه | *lait khestūwa* |
| etc. | etc. |

## THE CONDITIONAL

*Present*

"That" or "if I fall'

| SIMPLE VERB. | | COMPOUND INFINITIVE VERB. | |
|---|---|---|---|
| بكوم | *bīkawam* | لى بيخم | *lai bīkham* |
| بيكوى | *bīkawī* | لى بيخى | *lai bīkhaī* |
| بيكوه | *bīkawa* | لى بيخه | *lai bīkha* |
| بيكون | *bīkawin* | لى بيخن | *lai bīkhin* |
| بيكون | *bīkawin* | لى بيخن | *lai bīkhin* |
| بيكون | *bikawan* | لى بيخن | *lai bīkhan* |

### *Past*

"That" or "if I should fall"

| SIMPLE VERB. | | COMPOUND INFINITIVE VERB. | |
|---|---|---|---|
| بم کۆنوۆه | *bim kaotūwa* | لیم بخستوۆه | *laim bikhistūwa* |
| بت کۆتوۆه | *bit kaotūwa* | لیت بخستوۆه | *lait bikhistūwa* |
| بی کۆنوۆه | *bī kaotūwa* | لی بخستوۆه | *lai bikhistūwa* |
| بمان کۆتوۆه | *bimān kaotūwa* | لیمان بخستوۆه | *laimān bikhistūwa* |
| بتان ۆتوۆه | *bitān kaotūwa* | لیتان بخستوۆه | *laitān bikhistūwa* |
| بیان کۆتوۆه | *bīyān kaotūwa* | لییان بخستوۆه | *layān bikhistūwa* |

This is seldom heard, but it is encountered in poetry, and occasionally in oral translation of Turkish or Persian where the Kurd is rendering with exactitude the sense of the foreign language.

### *Imperative*

| | | | |
|---|---|---|---|
| بیکۆه | *bīkawa* | لیخه | *laikha* |
| بیکۆن | *bīkawin* | لیخن | *laikhin* |

The imperative may also take an initial *dābī* a word common to Sulaimania and Mukrī only, and renders the imperative more emphatic.

It also may be added to the conditional in the sense of certainty of occurrence of the action, as—

*dābī bīkawam* = that I shall certainly fall.
*dābī bībīstm* = that I shall certainly hear.

Such a phrase also has a purely future signification.

### *Future*

The future is usually formed by (1) use of *abī* = "it will become", (2) *-awa*, or (3) with both—

(1) *abī bīgūra* = he will change it.
(2) *daitawa* = he will come.
(3) *abī birūwa* = he will go.

The second is most generally employed. It is the present indicative + *-awa*, and is not heard in Hakkārī and Northern Kurmanjī.

They are all three obviously purely Kurdish uses, as there is no parallel to them either in Gūrān, Persian, or Lurish.

### *Past Participle*

There are two forms of this: (1) in *-ū* or *w*, (2) in *-rā*; the latter being a peculiar and novel feature of this branch of Kurdish.

One verb may use both these forms, as appears most convenient euphonically; for instance, from the verb *dān* appears *dāw* = "given", and in the perfect, "I have given," it would and does naturally occur as *-m dāwa*, but the second form may be, and often is, made use of, in some of which cases the pronominal particle is placed after the root thus: *dāmrā* = *dā* + *m* + *ra*, a formation of great peculiarity.

This occurs in a great many instances, and it may be taken that in the case of a verb whose root terminates in a vowel, the pronominal consonant precedes the *-rā* for the sake of avoiding a weak word like *dā* + *rā* + *m*, though this is quite a regular rule with all verbs whose roots end in a consonant; thus, from *kuzhdu*, past part. *kuzhrā*, perfect = *kuzhrām*, not *kuzhmrā*.

This formation in, and use of, *rā* appears to exist only in Sulaimania, for I never heard it in Hakkārī, Erbil, nor Mukrī.

The verb tables will show the verbs usually taking *-rā* in the past participle.

### *Infinitive Prefixes*

These are, as above remarked, so essential to many verbs, and have so little use apart from them, that they may be quoted here. The commonest are—

| | | |
|---|---|---|
| *hal,* | giving the meaning | back, up. |
| *lai* | ,, | destroying, crushing. |
| *tai* | ,, | in it, to it. |
| *rā* | ,, | movement. |
| *dā* | ,, | away, down. |
| *par* or *far* | ,, | out, away. |

Of these *hal* (the equivalent of the Persian *bar*) is by far the commonest.

### *Causative Form*

The Persian forms the causative by the insertion of *-ān* before the infinitive ending. The Mukrī and Sulaimania form by the same method, using the syllable *-īain*, as *irsiainin,* "to affright," from *tirsin,* "to fear," and so on.

### *Certain Peculiarities*

1. The language has almost lost the use of the verbs *dīn,* "to see," *paīā krdu,* "to find," and uses the first only in the 1st person singular preterite and perfect, *mdī* = "I saw", *mdīwa* = "I have seen", otherwise using the phrase *chao paī kaotn* = "the eyes falling upon" This signifies both seeing and finding.

2. In common with all Kurdish tongues, the verb "to have" does not exist, the sense being conveyed as in Turkish and Arabic = "to be", "to . . .", as—

> *pāra hayya la lāt?* = Hast thou money?
> Is there money to thee? (lit. at thy side).
>
> *Na, pārām niyya* = No, I have no money
> No, money to me is not.

3. There is only a relic of the verb "to want" "to wish", which is complete in Northern Kurdish, which gives *khāzin, wāzin,* etc.[1] Sulaimania, in colloquial language,

[1] As an example of how often Kurdish has produced, by its consonant and vowel changes, a word closely resembling English, we have the verb *wissin,* "to wish," in a middle dialect.

possesses no such verb, expressing its meaning by *haz krdn* = "to be pleased to".

4. Owing to the position and nature of the pronominal particle certain curious forms occur, where an objective pronoun is introduced; thus, in colloquial Persian the word *bibaram* has a meaning "take me away" or "take me", and can also be interpreted "I may take". Kurdish, however, avoids this ambiguity by a transposition, presenting for the first meaning—

*bīmba* = "take me".
*bī* = imperative prefix.
*-m-* = pronominal particle.
*-ba* = root "take".

*Bībam* would mean correctly and only "that I take". This use leads to such complications as—

*tadāīmī* = thou gavest it to me.
*ta* = thou.
*dāī* = gavest.
*m* = me.
*ī* = it.

Persian would have to use the analytic form *tū dādī ānrā bi man.*

It will be noticed that the Kurdish by this means produces a highly synthetic form. In the phrase *woutīshī* another peculiarity is observed—

*wout-* = he said.
*-īsh-* = also.
*-ī* = to him.

Persian presents *guftish ham,* but *ish* in Persian means "to him", not "also" as in Kurdish. This form in Kurdish is produced by the necessities of euphony, as *woutī-īsh* (the regular form) would allow the sense "to him" to disappear.

## List of Verbs

The 1st person singular of the various moods is quoted

| Infinitive. | Transliteration. | Pres. Ind. | Preterite. | Imperative. | Past Part. | English. |
|---|---|---|---|---|---|---|
| آفرین | *afirīn* (3rd pers. sing.) | دافره | آفری | | آفریو | to create |
| آگریان | *āgiriān* | آگریم | آگریام | آگریه | اگریو | to fire a cannon |
| ایشن | *aishn* (3rd pers. sing.) | أیشی | أیشی | | | to ache |
| بازدان | *bazdān* | see دان, *bāz* باز being prefixed | | | | to jump |
| بانگ کردن | *bañg kirdn* | see کردن, *bañg* being prefixed | | | | to call |
| بارین | *bārīn* | (3rd sing.) اباره | باری | | | to rain |
| بازین | *bāzīn* | دبازم | باری | | | to gamble |
| بچرین | *bichirrin* | ابچرم | ام بچری | بی بچری | بچرو | to pluck off |
| بخشین | *bakhshin* | ابخشم | ام بخشی | بی بخشه | بخشی | to excuse or grant |
| بردن | *birdn* | ایبم | ام برد | بی به | بردو | to take away |
| برّن | *birrin* | ایبرّم | ام برّی | بی برّ | بریؤ | to cut |
| بریان | *bariān* | بریم | بریمدا | بریه | بریاؤ | to release |
| بژیرن | *bzhairin* | ابژیرم | ام بژیری | بژیره | بژیرو | to exchange or give back |

| INFINITIVE. | TRANSLITERATION. | PRES. IND. | PRETERITE. | IMPERATIVE. | PAST PART. | ENGLISH. |
|---|---|---|---|---|---|---|
| بستن | *bastn* | ایبستم. | ام بست | بی بست | بستو | to bind |
| بون | *būn* | ابم | بوم | به | بود | to become |
| بین | *bīan* | ام | بوم | بی | بیه | to be |
| بیستن | *bīstn* | دبیستم | بستم | به بیست | بیستو | to hear |
| بیژن | *bīzhn* | ابیژم | ام بیژی | بی بیژد | بیژدا | to sift |
| پاره نیان | *pāra nīān* | see نیان , *pāra* being prefixed | | | | to push |
| پرسین | *pirsīn* | ایپرسم | ام پرسی | بی پرس | پرسیؤ | to ask |
| پر کوتن | *par kaotn* | see کوتن , *par* being prefixed | | | | to lie down |
| پک کوتن | *pak kaotn* | see کوتن , *pak* being prefixed | | | | to suffer loss or indignity |
| پیاچین | *paichin* | ایپیاچم | ام پیاچی | بی پیچ | پیاچیؤد | to twist |
| پینه کردن | *pīna kirdn* | see کردن , *pīna* being prefixed | | | | to patch |
| تراش کردن | *tarāsh kirdn* | see کردن , *tarāsh* being prefixed | | | | to shave the beard |
| ترسن | *tirsn* | اترسم | ام ترسی | بی ترسه | ترسیؤ | to fear |
| ترسیینن | *tirsiaīnin* | اترسیینم | ام ترسیین | بترسیین | ترسیینو | to affright |
| تکانن | *takānin* | اتکانم | ام تکانی | بیتکانه | تکانیؤ | to shake |
| تقانن | *taqānin* | اتقانم | ام تقانی | بی تقانه | تقانو | to fire a cannon |

| Infinitive. | Transliteration. | Pres. Ind. | Preterite. | Imperative. | Past Part. | English. |
|---|---|---|---|---|---|---|
| تکین | *takīn* (3rd sing.) | دتکی | اِی تکی | — | تکیۋ | to drip |
| ترشین | *turshīn* (3rd sing.) | دترشی | اِی ترشی | — | ترشیۋ | to become sour |
| برژان | *birzhan* (3rd sing.) | دبرژه | اِی برژا | — | برژاو | to be roasted |
| برژیمنن | *birzhiaīnin* | دبرژیینم | ام برژیین | بی برژیینه | برژیینو | to roast |
| تلاشین | *talāshīn* | دتلاشم | ام تلاشی | بیتلاشه | تلاشرا | to shave wood |
| تۋانن | *twānin* | اتۋانم | ام تۋانی | — | — | to be able |
| توریان | *tūrīān* | ایتورِم | توریام | — | توریاۋ | to quarrel |
| تی کردن | *tai kirdin* | see کردن, *tai* being prefixed | | | | to pour out |
| تی خستن | *tai khistn* | see خستن, *tai* being prefixed | | | | to pour, or throw into |
| تی گیشتن | *tai gaishtn* | see گیشتن, *tai* being prefixed | | | | to understand |
| تی یک بردن | *tai yek birdn* | see بردن, *tai* being prefixed | | | | to stir or mix |
| جوین | *jūīn* | ایجوم | ام جوی | بیجوه | جوۋ | to chew |
| جۋین | *jiwīn* | ایجۋم | ام جۋی | بیجۋه | — | to shake |
| جوش کردن | *jush kirdn* | see کردن, *jush* being prefixed | | | | to boil |
| جوش دان | *jush dān* | see دان; *jush* being prefixed | | | | to cause to boil |
| جیا کردن | *jīā kirdn* | see کردن, *jīā* being prefixed | | | | to separate |

| INFINITIVE. | TRANSLITERATION. | PRES. IND. | PRETERITE. | IMPERATIVE. | PAST PART. | ENGLISH. |
|---|---|---|---|---|---|---|
| جی اشتن | *jai ishtn* | جی ایلم | جیم اشت | جی ایله | جی اشتو | to leave, to set down |
| چسپینن | *chaspīainin* | اچسپینم | ام چسپیین | بی چپینه | چسپاۋ | to stick |
| چسپین | *chaspīn* (3rd sing.) | اچسپی | چسپی | بی چپه | چسپیۋ | to adhere |
| چمین | *chamīn* | ایچمی | ام چمی | بیچمه | چماۋ | to bend |
| چۋ ترکین | *chao tarkīn* | چۋ اترکم | چوم ترکی | چۋ بی ترکه | چو ترکاۋ | to wink |
| چون | *chūn* | اچم | چوم | بچو | چو | to go |
| چیشت کردن | *chaisht kirdn* | see کردن, *chaisht* being prefixed | | | | to cook |
| چیینن | *chīaīnin* | اچیینم | ام چیینی | بچیینه | چیینۋ | to plant |
| خرین | *khurīn* | ایخرم | ام خری | — | — | to irritate |
| خرینن | *khurainin* | ایخرینم | ام خرینی | بیخرینه | خریۋ | to scratch |
| خستن | *khistn* | دخم د خسم | ام خست | بخس | ختۋ | to throw |
| خسوتن | *khsūtn* | (3rd sing.) دخسو | خسوت | — | خسوۋ | to soak |
| خفتن | *khaftn* | دخفم | ام خفت | بیخف | خفتو | to go to sleep |
| خنکین | *khankīn* | اخنکم | ام خمکی | بخنکه | خنکو | to suffocate |
| خۋاردن | *khwārdin* | ایخۋم | ام خۋارد | بیخۋه | خۋاردو | to eat |
| خۋازن | *khwāzin* | دخۋازم | ام خۋازی | — | — | to want[1] |

[1] A defective verb, its parts are only used with عذر, to give the meaning "asking pardon," or "excusing oneself".

| INFINITIVE. | TRANSLITERATION. | PRES. IND. | PRETERITE. | IMPERATIVE | PAST PART. | ENGLISH. |
|---|---|---|---|---|---|---|
| خیونن | *khünin* | دخیونم | امخیونی | بیخیوین | خیونو | to read or sing |
| دانیشتن | *dānīshtn* | دانیشم | دامنیشت | دانشه | دانیشتو | to sit |
| دان | *dān* | ایم | امدا | بیه | داو | to give |
| دانیان | *dānīān* | see *nīān* نیان, *dā* being prefixed | | | | to put down |
| دا خستن | *dā khistn* | see *khistn* ختن, *dā* being prefixed | | | | to throw down |
| داگرسیینن | *dāgirsiainin* | داگرسیینم | داگرمسیینم | داگرسیینه | داگرسیینو | to light |
| درزی بردن | *dirzī birdn* | see *birdn* بردن, *dirzī* being prefixed | | | | to crack |
| درس کردن | *durus kirdn* | see *kirdn* کردن, *durus* being prefixed | | | | to make or put right |
| درو کردن | *drū kirdn* | see *kirdn* کردن. *drū* being prefixed | | | | to lie |
| درّین | *dirrīn* | ایدرّم | امدرّی | بیدرّه | درّاو | to tear |
| دزگرتن | *daz girtn* | see *girtn* گرتن, *daz* being prefixed | | | | to commence |
| دلوپه کردن | *dalaopa kirdn* | see *kirdn* کردن, *dalaopa* being prefixed | | | | to drip or leak |
| دورانن | *durānin* | ایدورم | امدوری | بیدوره | دوراو | to sew |
| دوشین | *dushin* | ایدوشم | امدوشی | بیدوشه | دوشرا | to milk |
| دین | *dīn* | — | امدی | — | دیو | to see (defective) |
| راز کردن | *rāz kirdn* | see *kirdn* کردن, *rāz* being prefixed | | | | to speak truth |

| INFINITIVE. | TRANSLITERATION. | PRES. IND. | PRETERITE. | IMPERATIVE. | PAST PART. | ENGLISH. |
|---|---|---|---|---|---|---|
| راز بون | *rāz būn* | see *būn* بون , *rāz* being prefixed | | | | to be content |
| را بردن | *rā birdn* | see *birdn* بردن , *rā* being prefixed | | | | to pass away (time) |
| را فرين | *rā farīn* | see *farīn* فرين , *rā* being prefixed | | | | to fly away |
| رّا ۋسان | *rrā wusān* | رّا ۋسم | رّام ۋسا | رّا ۋسه | رّا ۋساۋ | to stop, halt[1] |
| رّا كردن | *rrā kirdn* | see *kirdn* كردن , *rrā* being prefixed | | | | to flee |
| رّا چون | *rrā chūn* | see *chūn* چون , *rrā* being prefixed | | | | to hunt |
| رّاۋشين | *rrā wushīn* | رّا ۋشم | رّام ۋشى | رّاۋشه | رّاۋشو | to roll |
| رزين | *razīn* | (3rd sing.) ارزى | رزى | — | رزيۋ | to rot |
| رسين | *risīn* | ارسم | امرسى | برسه | رسيۋ | to spin |
| رشان | *rishān* | درشم | امرشى | برشه | رشاۋ | to vomit |
| رنبازن | *runbāzin* | ارنبازم | امرنبازى | درنباز | رنبازيۋ | to gallop |
| روخان | *rūkhān* | (3rd sing.) دروخه | روخا | روخه | روخاۋ | to stumble (an animal) |
| رونق دان | *rūniq dān* | see *dān* دان , *rūniq* being prefixed | | | | to sparkle |
| رو هشتن | *ru hishtn* | رو هيلم | رو هشتم | — | روهشتو | to start on the road |
| رّوين | *rrūīn* | اروم | امرّوى | برّو | رّوۋ | to go |

[1] Although this is but *rrā* prefixed to *wusān*, it is given here thus, as *wusān* is never used alone.

| Infinitive. | Transliteration. | Pres. Ind. | Preterite. | Imperative. | Past Part. | English. |
|---|---|---|---|---|---|---|
| ریژن | *raizhin* | دریژم | امریژی | بریژه | ریژاو | to pour |
| ریوخینن | *rükhainin* | اریوخینم | امروخینی | بروخینه | روخینو | to shatter (a house) |
| زاین | *zāin* | ازیم | امزا | بیزا | زارا | to give birth |
| زانن | *zānin* | دزانم | امزانی | بزان | — | to know |
| ژمردن | *zhmirdan* | اژمرم | امژیرد | بی‌ژمر | ژمردو | to count |
| سنک کردن | *siñ̃g kirdn* | see *ꝁirdn* کردن, *siñ̃g* being prefixed | | | | to hang up |
| سوتن | *sūtn* | اسوتم | امسوتی | بیسوته | سوترا | to burn |
| سوتانن | *sūtānin* | اسوتانم | امسوتان | بیسوتان | سوتانو | to cause to burn |
| سییندن | *siaindn* | دسیینم | امسیینی | بسیینه | — | to buy, get |
| شتن | *shtn* | ایشوم | امشت | بیشو | شتاو | to wash |
| شرقینن | *sharqainin* | اشرقینم | امشرقیین | بشرقین | شرقینو | to confuse |
| شکاون | *shkāwan* | اشکاوم | امشکاو | بی‌شکاو | شکاو | to unpick |
| شکان | *shikān* | اشکام | امشکا | بی‌شکا | شکاو | to break |
| شکیان | *shikīān* | (3rd sing ) ایشکد | شکیا | — | — | to break (intransitive) |
| شییلین | *shiailin* | اشییلم | امشییلی | بشییله | — | to massage or rub |
| فرمون | *farmūn* | (3rd sing.) افرمو | فرمو | بفرمو | فرموو | to command |

| INFINITIVE. | TRANSLITERATION. | PRES. IND. | PRETERITE. | IMPERATIVE. | PAST PART. | ENGLISH. |
|---|---|---|---|---|---|---|
| فروشتن | *frūshtin* | ابفروشم | ام فروشتی | بیفروشه | فروشتو | to sell |
| فرّین | *farrīn* | افرّم | ام فرّی | بیفرّه | فرّیڤ | to fly |
| فره دان | *fara dān* | see *dān* دان, *fāra* being prefixed | | | | to throw away |
| قت کردن | *qat kirdn* | see *kirdn* کردن, *qat* being prefixed | | | | to fold |
| قرقش کردن | *qirqish kirdn* | see *kirdn* کردن, *qirqish* being prefixed | | | | to wind a watch |
| قی کردن | *qai kirdn* | see *kirdn* کردن, *qai* being prefixed | | | | to be concerned |
| کردن | *kirdn* | ایکم | ام کرد | بیکه | کردو | to do |
| کردن آوا | *kirdn āwā* | ایکم آوا / ایکمو | کردم آوا / کردمو | بیکرو | کردڤا | to open |
| کرّین | *kirrīn* | دکرّم | ام کرّی | بیکر | کرّیڤ | to buy |
| کشان | *kishān* | ایکشم | ام کشا | بیکش | کشرا | to draw, suffer, sustain |
| کشانوا | *kushān awā* | کُشوا | کشانو | — | — | to open (a bud) |
| کلانن | *klānin* | ایکلم | ام کلا | بیکلا | کلاڤ | to cook |
| کندن | *kandin* | ایکنم | ام کند | بیکن | کندڤ | to excavate |
| کنن | *kunin* | دکنم | ام کنی | بکن | — | to laugh |
| کوتن | *kaotn* | اکوم | ام کوت | بیکوه | کوتو | to fall |

| INFINITIVE. | TRANSLITERATION. | PRES. IND. | PRETERITE. | IMPERATIVE. | PAST PART. | ENGLISH. |
|---|---|---|---|---|---|---|
| کوتن | *kūtin* | ایکوم | ام کوت | بیکو | کوترا | to pound |
| کوژدن | *kūzhdin* | ایکوژم | ام کوژد | بیکوژه | کوژدا | to kill or extinguish |
| گازگرتن | *gāz girtn* | see *girtn* گرتن, *gāz* being prefixed | | | | to bite |
| گاهن | *gāhin* | اگمم | ام گا | بیگا | گارا | to rape or spoil |
| گرتن | *girtn* | ایگرم | ام گرت | بیگره | گرتو | to seize |
| گرّیان | *garrīān* | ایگرّم | ام گرّی | بیگرّه | گرّیاڤ | to wander |
| گوتن | *gūtin* | — | ام گوت | — | گوتو | to speak |
| گورن | *gūrin* | ایگورم | ام گوری | بیگور | گوراو | to exchange |
| گیرین | *gīrīn* | ایگیرم | ام گیری | بیگیره | (گیریڤ) | to weep |
| گیشتن | *gaishtin* | ایگیم | ام گیشت | — | گیشتو | to arrive |
| لاچون | *lāchūn* | see *chūn* چون, *lā* being prefixed | | | | to go out |
| لاڤان | *lāwān* | | لاڤام | لاوا | — | to take off |
| لبیر چون | *labīr chūn* | see *chūn* چون, *lā* being prefixed | | | | to forget |
| لڤارن | *lwārin* | (3rd sing.) الڤاری | لڤاری | بیلڤاره | — | to graze |
| لڤارینن | *lwārainin* | الڤارینم | لڤارینم | بیلڤارینه | | to cause to graze |
| لن | *ḷn* or *iḷn* | ایلم | ام الی | بیله | — | to speak |

| INFINITIVE. | TRANSLITERATION. | PRES. IND. | PRETERITE. | IMPERATIVE. | PAST PART. | ENGLISH. |
|---|---|---|---|---|---|---|
| لی خستن | *lai khistn* | see *khistn* خستن , *lai* being prefixed | | | | to strike |
| لی دان | *lai dān* | see *dān* دان , *lai* being prefixed | | | | to strike very hard |
| لی کردن | *lai kirdn* | see *kirdn* کردن , *lai* being prefixed | | | | to press |
| لی یک کردن | *lai yek kirdn* | see *kirdn* کردن , *lai yek* being prefixed | | | | to mix |
| مردن | *mirdin* | ایمرم | میردم | بمیره | مردو | to die |
| ماٶن | *māwn* | امیمیم | مام | بمیینه | ماٶ | to remain |
| ٶیستن | *mwīstn* | اموی | امٶیست | — | — | to wish [1] |
| ناسن | *nāsin* | اینماسم | ام ناسی | بی ناس | ناسو | to recognize |
| نوسان | *nūisān* | انوسم | ام نوست | بی نوس | نوسرا | to write |
| نٶستن | *nwistan* | انوم | ام نٶست | بنسٶه | نوستو | to sleep |
| نیان | *nīān* | انم | ام نیا | بنه | نیاد | to allow |
| نیردن | *nairdin* | انیرم | ام نیرد | بنیر | نیردو | to send |
| ٶا هاتن | *wā hātin* | see *hātin* هاتن, *wā* being prefixed | | | | to return |
| ٶا گرتن | *wā girtn* | see *girtn* گرتن, *wā* being prefixed | | | | to cause to return, to overturn |
| ٶوتن | *wūtn* | ایژم | امٶوت | بیژه | ٶوتو | to speak |

[1] Now obsolete.

| INFINITIVE. | TRANSLITERATION. | PRES. IND. | PRETERITE. | IMPERATIVE. | PAST PART. | ENGLISH. |
|---|---|---|---|---|---|---|
| هاتن | *hātin* | دیم | هاتم | وَرَه | هاتوو | to come |
| هشتن | *hishtin* | ایلم | امهشت | بیله | هشتو | to allow |
| هل وسیین | *hal wushiainin* | هل وشیینم | هلم وسیینی | هل وشیینه | هل وسیینو | to scatter about |
| هل پیاچیینن | *hal pīchiainin* | هل پیاچیینم | هلم پیاچیینی | هل پیاچیینه | هل پیاچیو | to roll up cloth |
| هل بچین | *hal behīn* | هل ابچم | هلم بچیی | هل بچی | هل بچیو | to unpick |
| هل فترین | *hal farrīn* | see *farrīn*, *hal* being prefixed | | | | to jump |
| هل سان | *hal sān* | هل سم | هل سام | هل سَه | هل ساو | to rise on the feet |
| هل گرتن | *hal girtn* | see *girtn*, *hal* being prefixed | | | | to take up |
| هل گتریان | *hal garrīān* | see *garrīān*, *hal* being prefixed | | | | to come back |
| هل تکانن | *hal takānin* | see *takānin*, *hal* being prefixed | | | | to shake out |
| هل بژاردن | *hal bzhārdin* | see *bzhārdin*, *hal* being prefixed | | | | to choose |
| هل پرین | *hal parīn* | هل اپرم | هلم پری | هل پرّه | هل پریو | to leap |
| هل وستن | *hal wustn* | هل اوستم | هلم وست | هل وستة | هل وساو | to hang up |
| هونن | *hunin* | ایهونم | امهون | بیهون | هونیو | to spin |
| هیینن | *hīaīnin* | اهیینم / دهیینم | هینام / امهینا | بیآینه | هیناو | to bring |

## PRONOUNS

These are as simple as in Persian, and possess no inflexions for case. Unlike the extreme Northern Kurmānjī the 1st person singular presents the same form as Persian, for the Bayazid and Erzerum dialects give *az*.

| | | | | | |
|---|---|---|---|---|---|
| I | من | *min*, | We | ايمه | *aima*, |
| Thou | تو or اتو | *tū* or *atū*, | You | ايوه | *aiwa*, |
| He, she, it | آو | *āw*, | They | اوان | *awān*, |

with the reflexives—

| | | | |
|---|---|---|---|
| Myself | خوم | *khwam* | = *khwa* + *am*. |
| Thyself | خوت | *khwat* | = *khwa* + *t*. |
| Himself | خوى | *khwuī* | = *khwa* + *ī*. |
| Ourselves | خومان | *khwamān* | = *khwa* + *amān*. |
| Yourselves | خوتان | *khwatān* | = *khwa* + *atān*. |
| Themselves | خويان | *khwayān* | = *khwa* + *ayān* |

The possessive is formed by adding one of the words -*ī*, *hī*, or *hīn*, usually the last, making—

*hīn-ī-mīn* = mine.
*hīn-ī-tū* = thine, etc.

The Persianized form *māl-ī-min* is seldom heard.

The dative and objective forms are usually affixed to verbs when possible, as in Persian, and give the following regular forms (though the position may change according to the requirements of euphony)—

| | | | |
|---|---|---|---|
| *tadā* + *m* | = | thou gavest | + to me. |
| *dā* + *t* | = | he gave | + to thee. |
| *mdā* + *ī* | = | I gave | + to him. |
| *dā* + *mān* | = | he gave | + to us. |
| *mdā* + *tān* | | I gave | + to you. |
| *mdā* + *yān* | = | I gave | + to them. |

The objective form becomes obscure in such cases as—

*lai* + *m* + *t* + *dā*, thou struckest me.
*lai* + *t* + *m* + *dā*, I struck thee.
*lai* + *ī* + *m* + *dā*, I struck him.
*lai* + *mān* + *ī* + *dā*, he struck us.
*lai* + *tān* + *m* + *dā*, I struck you.
*lai* + *yān* + *m* + *dā*, I struck them

All these, however, show the perfect regularity of the Kurdish pronominal form, as the terminations and prefixes of the verbal forms are identical, except for the last three persons in the present indicative, "we, you, they go," all represented by final *n*, *ach*, + *n*. Here the first syllable of the plural forms has disappeared, leaving only a final -*n*. This is a distinctive feature of Middle and Northern Kurdish, which presents the same form.

*Demonstrative pronouns* are as in North and Middle Kurdish, which give أو and ۆ = "this" and "that". Sulaimania has preserved the original *m* in the first of these words, giving ام (Zend *aem*). The plurals مانه and اوانه give "these" and "those".

*Interrogatives* چه, كه, كام. The first have the same interrogative and conjunctive use as in Persian. كام is the Persian كدام.

### Adverbs, Prepositions, etc.

The commonest of these are as follows—

| | | |
|---|---|---|
| له | *la* | from, at, a word in use wherever Kurdish is spoken |
| باى | *bāī* | for, at, as in باى چن, "at what price," a local Sulaimania word |
| پى | *pai* | to, as in پيم ۆوتى, *paim wouti*, "he said to me" |

| | | |
|---|---|---|
| بو | *bo* | for, to, as بومن, "for me"; کرکوک "to Kirkūk" |
| لگل | *lagal* | with, as وره لگلی خوم, *waira lagalī khwam* = come with me |
| با | *bā* | together with |
| بی | *baī* | without |
| لنو | *lanaw* | in, *nāw* being "the interior" |
| تی | *tuī* | in, i.e. "at the bottom" |
| لسر | *lasar* | on top of |
| لژیر | *lazhīr* | under |
| لپشت | *lapisht* | behind |
| لور | *lawar* | before; *war* is common Kurdish, now signifying "in front", "forward" |
| خوار | *khwār* | down, low |
| بان | *bān* | up, high |
| لبر | *labar* | by reason of |
| پیش | *paish* | in front |
| دواو | *duwāw* | at the back of |
| لشون<br>شون | *lashūn*<br>*shūn* | in pursuit of, behind |
| جاران | *jārān* | formerly |
| جار | *jār* | a time |
| جارک | *jārek* | once |
| ایسته | *īsta* | now |
| آو وخت | *āw wakht* | then |
| لوی | *lawai* | here |
| لوره | *laūra* | there |
| هیره | *haira* | here |
| هر جی | *har jai* | wherever |
| همو جی | *hamu jai* | everywhere |

| | | |
|---|---|---|
| هیچ جی | *hīch jai* | nowhere |
| لکو | *lakụ?* | where? |
| چلون | *chlūn* | how (from Arabic اشلون) |
| چون | *chūn?* | how? |
| ڤا | *wā* | thus |
| امجار | *amjār* | this time |
| بشکه | *bashki* | perhaps |
| قد | *qadd* | certainly (Sulaimania town only, from Arabic) |
| درنگ | *drañg* | late |
| زو | *zū* | early |
| توزک | *tụzek* | in a little while |
| یکجار | *yekjār* | suddenly |
| چن | *chan?* | how much? how many? |
| چنی | *chanī?* | how much? how often? |
| باش | *bāsh* | well, good |
| چاک | *chāk* | well, good |
| هر | *har* | every, always, ever |
| نا | *nā* | no |
| بری | *barī* | yes (often pronounced *mbarī*) |
| للا | *lalā* | towards, with |
| ڤکو | *wakū* | like, resembling |
| تا | *tā* | as far as |
| هنی | *hanī* | as yet |
| انجاخ | *anjākh* | hardly (Turkish انجق) |
| زور | *zūr* | very |
| جاریتر | *jārītir* | again |
| اش | *ish* | also |
| بوچی | *bụchī?* | why? |
| بو | *bụ?* | why? |

## POETRY

The following are some verses by Mustafa Beg, whose pen-name was Hajarī Kurdī, who wrote about 1815–20 A.D.

The verse form is the commonest of Kurdish poetry couplets, the first two or three of the poem rhyming both lines, the subsequent verses rhyming only the last line with the first verses.

There is much more Persian in the verse than in the spoken language, and Arabic words are widely employed.

1. تالانی سر و مالم چاوی رش فتانت
پی بندی دلو دینم کاکول پریشانت

*Tālānī sar u mālim chaoī rash i fattānat*
*Pai bandī diḷū dīnim kākul i parishānit.*

My head and house are captives of thy seductive black eyes.
My heart and faith are bound to thy bewitching coiffure.

*Tālānī* = "the captive of a raid".

*Kākul i parishānit.* The *kākul*, or cock's comb, is used to denote in poetry the headgear of a woman, which, among the outside people and villagers, is often a large turban of many coloured silk handkerchiefs.

2. *Gharamat aya bo am diḷ ruswām bikai wa girdit.*
*Dassit haligirra laim ītr sā khwat bī wa īmānit.*

Thou art enraged against this heart, thou wilt shame me before thee.
Remove, then, thy hand from me; be your own faith to yourself (i.e. keep your love to yourself).

*Aya* = "it comes"; *ītr*, Persian *dīgar* = "then", "again"; *wa girdit* = "around", "before thee"; *sā*, "now."

*bī* = "be"

3. *Waku khanjar zī jaushan tā ruzhī hashar datakī.*
*Khūn i diḷ mazlūwān law nawki mizhgānit.*

Like a heart-stabbing dagger, till the last day may there drip
The blood of oppressed hearts from within thy lashes.

*Datakī* is pres. indic. of *takīn*, "to drip."

Below is one of a few rubāiyāt of Nālī, the most celebrated Sulaimanian poet, a Kurd, of Panjwīn, who died about 1870. His poems cover a great variety of subjects, metre, and form, comprising *ghazaliyyāt*, a *ḥajw* on himself, a very fine *marthīyya*, a *tarjī'band*, and several *qaṣida*. He has also written a large number of *gūrānī*, a Kurdish form, where the first line is sung by one man, and the two or three words comprising the second line are repeated in chorus by the rest of those present.

*Lao sāwa nūr i dīdaka chāwam birrīwa min*
*Bụ hātinit laraiwa ki chāwam birrīwa min*
*Hāīl nāmā labarī, pai tū dīda mā*
*Farmū ki pardakai sabalam har birrīwa min.*

From then, that my eyes' light was cut from my sight,
I wore my eyes awaiting her return from the road,
So that when no screen hid her (i.e. at last she came) my sight for her had lasted.
She said: "I have torn away for ever from thee my life's curtain."

A chorus song or gūrānī. The accented syllables are sung with great emphasis, and are marked —

1. *Dastī́ bīa wa dás i shakáwam ki bi sár chūm*
   *Qurbā́ni* *vefū́tm*
2. *Tū Yū́sifi nō húsn la sar misir khubā́nī*
   *Min pī́ri* *mufā́nī*
3. *Farqī́ki nakárd nafs nafī́sm bizā́yat*
   *Wahshī́ la* *vilā́yat*
4. *Lam kū́shai waīrā́nīa har mā́mawa wa kábūm*
   *Wai sháwam* *walā́tm*

I give the Persian equivalent of these verses, as supplying a better explanation in a smaller space than English—

دستی بده بدست شکستم که هلاک شدم
قربان وفای توهستنم
تویوسف نوحسن ازسر مصر خبان[1]
مَن پیر موفانی

[1] From خبانیدن " to trample down ".

هیچ تفاوتی نکردای نفس غزیزم بحالت
این وحشی از دور
از آن گوشهٔ خراب شده همشد مانده بودم در جای خودم
امّا اشب پهلوی توهستم

The following is one of the few specimens of prose encountered, a letter written by a Kurd to the writer while living in Sulaimania as a Persian. English literation is given with Persian under it—

*Buzurgavār āmirzā ghulām Husain i fārsī, khizmatm.*
*Buzurgavār agha mirza Ghulam Husain i īrānī, khidmatam.*

*Pash i arz das busī ahvālakānit,*
*Pas az arz i dast būsī va ahvālat,*
After kissing thy hand and asking thy health,

*khwā shukur wa salāmatm gaisht la Halabja.*
*khudā shukr bā salamat rasīdam bi Alabja.*
God thanks with safety I arrived to Halabja.

*nāzānam o maktūb ī khwam ki nuisrām gaishtawa*
*namīdānam ān maktub i khudam ki navishta am rasīda ast.*
I know not that letter of myself that I have written is arrived

*yā na Dīyār ī rūn ī Sayyid Ali Ababailī hātawa.*
*yā khair. Khabar i rūghan i Sayyid Ali Abā 'Ubaidī āmada ast.*
or not. News of the rūghan of Sayyid Ali Ababaili is come.

*Hama wa Makha daln rūnimān niyya, wa*
*Ahmad va Mikail mignyand rūghan nadarim, va*
Ahmad and Mikail say our rūghan is not, and

*Khwāja Mansūrish rūī bo Tawīla. Hagar haz dakai*
*Khāja Mansūr ham raft bi Tavīla. Agar mīkhāhī*
Khāja Mansūr also went to Tavīla. If you desire

*rūnaka bisīainī āgām ka tā bīnuism bo*
*rūghan bigīrī āgāh-am kun ta binavīsam bi*
rūghan to get advise me till I write to

*Khwāja Mansūr. pāra la Makha bisiaīna, wa*
*Khwāja Mansūr, pūl az Mikail bigīrad, va*
Khwāja Mansūr, money from Mikail may take, and

*rūnaka bikirra Ista shash bār rūn lawai*
*rūghan bikharad. Hālā shish bār rūghan injā*
rūghan may buy. Now six loads rūghan here

*hayyatī dafarūshn, walī tama i Makha zūra,*
*hast-ash mifurūshand, valī ṭama' i Mikail khaili ast,*
it is they sell, but greed of Mikail is much,

*wa khwaī zūr pīska-a. Itir hīn ī bāzargānīm*
*va khudash khailī mumsik ast. Digar mal i tijārati*
and himself very mean is. Then that of merchandise I

*hainā bīgūram bo rūn yā na, hagar hatī*
*āvurdam avaz kunam bā rūghan yā khair, agar*
brought may I change for rūghan or not, if

*bzhairam māl ī chākish hayya, wa pārām*
*tamīz bidiham chīz-i-khūb hast, va pūlam*
I pick out that [which] of goodness also is, and my money

*hayya lalāī kābarāek lawai. Mansūr dalai dū so*
*hast pīshi yak kasi injā. Mansūr mignyad davist*
is with one so-and-so here. Mansūr says two hundred

*tahrānīa kaoshakānish zūram furushtī, qazānjish*
*qirān ast kafsh-ha ham khailī furukhtam. manfa'at ham*
qirāns is The shoes also much I sold, profit too

*kirdawa. Ish wakū jārān haira niyya.*
*karda ast. Kār misl pīshtar injā nīst.*
is made. Affairs like formerly here are not.

*khwā bika Hamavand blao ben bāsh abī.*
*khudā bikunad Hamavand bar taraf shavand khūb mīshavad.*
God do the Hamavand scatter well it will become.

*Itir dānishtm bo farmānit*
*Digar nishastam barāyī farmāyish-at*
Further I sat for thy commands.

HAMA I MUKRĪ.
AHMAD THE MUKRĪ.

7 *Rajab*, 1327.

# A SOUTHERN KURDISH FOLKSONG IN KERMANSHAHI DIALECT

By E. B. SOANE

THE Kurdish dialect of Persian has so far received very little attention from Oriental students, though it fully merits study, for while actually nothing more than a Persian dialect it has not submitted to the erosion which time brings about in every language, and which is so marked a feature in the development of modern Persian. Nor has it been subject to that admixture of Arabic words which has become so great a part of Persian since the invasion of the early Muhammadan Arabs. As a consequence it has preserved intact many words now obsolete in the mother language. Preserved from foreign influence, both by the rude and savage nature of the Kurds and by the inaccessibility of their mountainous homes, the Kurdish tongues (for there are many dialects) present an almost fundamentally pure Persian dialect, though much spoiled by corruption in pronunciation and the abbreviation always accompanying this feature of a language.

Some attention has been bestowed upon Kurdish by Russian scholars within the last four decades, but the dialects brought under notice have been those of the extreme north, notably Kermanji and the dialects of Buyazid in the eastern Caucasus, which show very considerable differences from those of the southern Kurds, who exist as far as Kermanshah, a linear distance of some four hundred miles from their most northerly kinsmen.

Generally speaking, the great belt of high mountain

lands stretching from the extreme north-west in a wide crescent to the south of Persia has been the conservatory of the old tongue, which in various gradations is found among the wild inhabitants of this region, from the large race of Kurds through Bakhtiārī, Lurī—northern and southern — Kāzerūni in Fars, Dashtistānī, Tangistānī, Minābī to the confines of the Baluch country, each of which forms a connecting link between its northern and southern neighbours in the same way as do the sub-dialects of Kurdish to those around them.

The dialect here exemplified, as being the most southerly, shows many features which are essentially Kurdish, and many again both common to Kurd and Lur. As the poem here presented is in the Kurdish of to-day, any reference to a Persian word as being obsolete will be to modern colloquial Persian, thus affording a true comparison between modern Kurdish and Persian.

The song is one heard at every gathering in Kermanshah. Its metre is, as is the case with all such poetry, very simple, and varying in some couplets. As the rhyme is confined to the two halves of the couplet, not extending to the preceding and following lines, any number may be added at the will of the singer, and this is in practice very often done. The poem is known as "Qaṭār-i-Kurdī", *qatār* being a usual name for any long series of couplets.

1. **Khiāl parkanda,[1] dil tarfītūnam[2]**
   **Chūn Farhād, shāhid[3] i Bisītūnam.**

Of thoughts scattered, my heart is distressed;
Like Farhad, martyr of Bisitūn, am I.

2. Khiālī makai[1] la[2] tū dūram
   Mar[3] mirdin[4] buwait[5] nāmit la wīram.[6]

Think not that I am far from thee
Unless death take thy name from my memory.

---

COUPLET 1.

[1] *parkanda,* equivalent of Persian *parāganda, parākanda,* "scattered," "dispersed."

[2] *tarfītūn* (*ū* pronounced as German *ü*), "distressed," from the Kurdish verb *tarfitūnin,* "to be distressed;" *am* is the 1st singular present indicative of the verb "to be".

[3] *shāhid,* signifying a martyr, from the usage of *shāhid* in connection with the Shi'ah martyrs Husain and Hasan, commonly termed *shāhid* in colloquial Persian.

The last line refers to the well-known tradition of Farhad, who attempted the demolition of the Bisitūn Mountain near Kermanshah in order to gain the hand of Shirīn.

COUPLET 2.

[1] *makai,* Persian *makun,* 'do not."

[2] *la,* Persian *az,* "from."

[3] *mar, magar,* "unless."

[4] *mirdin,* Persian *murdan,* "to die," or verbal noun, "dying."

[5] *buwait,* Persian *bibarad,* "that it take." Kurdish infinitive *birdin,* the root *bir* having been corrupted to *wa,* as with the same verb in Luri and southern mountain dialects.

[6] *wīram* = *wīr* + *am,* "my memory." Cf. Ar. *wīr,* "the mind."

3. Wa [1] maīlī yārān qarīb i dil rīsh
Wa giān [2] i Kishbar wa Sāmeranīsh.[3]

By the love of friends near the heart's wound,
By the soul of Kishbar in her Sāmera.

4. Wārān [1] buwārit [2] batīa [3] bakai [4] tar
Wa Sāmera chīm [5] wa māl [6] i Kishbar.

Let the rain rain and wet my cheek.
I go to Sāmera, to the house of Kishbar.

---

### Couplet 3.

[1] *wa*, Persian *bi*, the *bāyi qasam*, "preceding an oath."

[2] *giān*, Persian *jān*, "the soul." *Giān i Kishbar*, "soul of Kishbar," which is a common Kurdish name for a woman.

[3] *Sāmeranīsh* = *Sāmera* + *n* + *īsh*. *Sāmera*, the allusion to a beauty of Samera of Turkestan ; *-ish*, a possessive termination not necessary to the sense. The medial *-n-* is purely euphonic.

### Couplet 4.

[1] *wārān*, Persian *bārān*, "rain."

[2] *buwārit*, Persian *bibārad*, "let it rain."

[3] *batīa*, "a cloak."

[4] *bakai*, Persian *bikunad*, "let it make."

[5] *chīm*, "I go," from Kermanshahi *chīan*, "to go," a survival of the ancient *chīū*, "going."

[6] *māl*, the Kurdish use for a house.

5. **Māl i dūs bār kird wa nā rezā i dil**
**Allah yārī [1] būt [2] manzil wa manzil.**

**The friend's steed they loaded with unwilling heart**
**God be his friend from stage to stage.**

6. **Bichīm [1] wa jākai [2] Farhād i kihinakan [3]**
**Bidaīm [4] wa sardā [5] rīza i pāra i sang.**

**Let us go to the place of Farhād the mountain-breaker**
**And strike our heads with fragments of stone.***

* i.e. in grief for the friend's departure.

---

COUPLET 5.

[1] *yārī*, Persian *yār-ash* = "his friend." Kermanshāhī uses -*i* in place of the Persian genitive termination -*ash*, "of him, her, it."

[2] *būt*, Persian *bāshad*, "may he be," from infinitive *bīan*, "to be."

COUPLET 6.

[1] *bichīm*, "let us go;" see note 5 to couplet 4.

[2] *jāka* = Persian *jā*, "a place."

[3] *kihinakan*, Persian *kūhān kan*, the breaker of mountains.

[4] *bidaīm*, "let us strike," from *dān*, "to strike," root *da*.

[5] *sardā*, Persián *sar*, "head," or "heads". The affix -*da* occurs in Kurdish nouns; usually placed in an objective or a noun preceded by a preposition.

7. Agar Musalmānī rām [1] la [2] jāmita [3]
Zardi o zaīfīm [4] paī [5] shamāmita.[6]

If thou be a Musulman, mercy is in thy garments.
My pallor and weakness are because of thy delicacy.

8. Yeh [1] chi dardi bī,[2] bī wa duchāram
Sar bī wa sālār,[3] lash [4] bī [5] wa bāram.

What malady was this, it was from our meeting.
My brain is swelled, my body dead with my load (of love).

---

COUPLET 7.

[1] *rām*, Persian *raḥm*, "mercy."

[2] *la*, Persian *bi*, *az*, *dar*, "in."

[3] *jāmita* = *jām-at-ast*, "is in thy garments."

[4] *zaīfīm* = Persian *zaīfī-yi-man* (ضعيفى), "my weakness."

[5] *paī*, "for," "because of." This is still used as most Persian dialects and in old Persian.

[6] *shamāmita* = *shamām-at-ast*, "thy delicacy is."

COUPLET 8.

[1] *yeh* = Persian *īn*, "this."

[2] *bī*, Persian *būd*, "was;" the past tense used in a present sense, as is common both in Kurdish and vulgar Persian.

[3] *sālār*, "swelled."

[4] *lash*, Persian *lāsh*, "dead," "a corpse."

[5] *bīm*, Persian *shudam*, "I became." The Kurds have no proper distinction between the verbs "to be" and "to become".

9. Nīshī[1] wa zhangit[2] manīt[3] wa jarda[4]
Manīt wa sepāi tāzeh fatḥ karda.

Thy lashes and eyebrows are like a robber,
Like an army newly come from victory.*

* The metaphor is that of the lashes and eyebrows being like the lances and bows of an army.

10. Cha bikam[1] wa dast i yeh naō namāma[2]
Shaō[3] la pazhāraī[4] khaō[5] l'īm[6] ḥarāma.

What can I do at the hand of this fresh beauty?
At night, from thought of her, sleep is forbidden me.

---

COUPLET 9.

1 *nīshī*, "eyelashes," Persian *muzha*.
2 *zhangit*, "thy eyebrows."
3 *manīt*, Persian *mimānad*, idiom for "resembles".
4 *jarda*, "a robber."

COUPLET 10.

1 *bikam*, Persian *bikunam*, "may I do."
2 *naō namāma*, "fresh beauty."
3 *shaō*, Persian *shab*, "night."
4 *pazhāraī*, "prepossession of her," "thoughts of her."
5 *khaō*, Persian *khwāb*, "sleep."
6 *l'īm* = *la* + *ī* + *am*, Persian *az man*, "from me." The junction of the two short *a*'s in *la* and *am* usually produces in Kurdish one long *ī* sound

11. Ham kaft[1] wa wīram[2] khāsī[3] yi Shaukat
Shīrīnī yī annām[4] zhīr i kulkwat.[5]

Also fell to my mind the goodness of Shaukat,
The sweetness of her figure under her tunic.

12. Khānum khānumān bān[1] wa 'amārat
Wa pām mashq makat,[2] wa chaō[3] ishārat.

The lady of ladies upon her housetop
Dances for me with her feet, and beckons with her eyes.

---

Couplet 11.

[1] *kaft*, "fell," from Kurdish verb *kaftin*, "to fall."

[2] *wīram*, "my memory." See note 6, couplet 2.

[3] *khāsī*, "goodness," Arabic خاصّ. The Persian word *khūb* is seldom used in Kurdish.

[4] *annām*, obsolescent Persian *andām*, "form," "stature."

[5] *kulkwat*, the Kurdish woman's garment, a kind of tunic, with full pleated skirts, also called *kulanja* and *kamarchīn*.

Couplet 12.

[1] *bān*, Persian *bām* and *bāla*, "up," "above."

[2] *wa pām mashq makat*, a Kurdish idiom for the Persian *bā pā mashq mīkunad barāyi man*. This occurs but rarely, however, in such an involved phrase. In some Persian dialects the sentence, while preserving the same idea of a possessive pronominal termination instead of a separate pronoun and preposition, would read *bā pā mashqam mīkunad*.

[3] *chaō*, Persian *chashm*, "eyes."

13. Dam[1] gird a mam[2] gird, pisht i pāshna[3] gird
Masī[4] yi chaōwakat[5] min[6] la dunyā bird.

Round mouth, round breast, round heel,
Intoxication of thy eyes took me from this world.

14. Har chan[1] manīshim[2] sāl dumātir[3]
Khwashīm[4] kam maü[5] talkhīm zīātir.[6]

The longer I remain succeeding years .
My pleasure decreases, my bitterness grows more.

---

### Couplet 13.

[1] *dam*, Persian *dahan*, "mouth."

[2] *mam*, "the breast." Though no recognized Persian, equivalent exists, the words *mimeh*, *mām*, and one or two other variants occur in the same sense in the South Persian and Lur dialects.

[3] *pisht i pāshna*, Persian *pusht i pāshneh*, "the heel."

[4] *masī*, Persian *mastī*, "intoxication."

[5] *chaōwakat* = *chaō* + *ak* + *at*, "thy eyes." The termination -*ak* is as common in Kurdish as in vulgar Persian for all nouns.

[6] *min*, Persian *man*, "me," "I."

### Couplet 14.

[1] *har chan*, Persian *har chand*, "however much."

[2] *manīshim*, Persian *mīnishīnam*, "I sit," "remain." The verbal form with initial *m* is hardly correct Kermanshāhī, which as a rule omits any prefix in present indicative.

[3] *dumātir* = Persian *dumbāltar*, "later," "more behind." The word *dumbāl* is now little used except in the dialects of Yazd and Isfahan.

[4] *khwashīm*, Persian *khūshī-am*, "my pleasure."

[5] *maü*, Persian *mīshavad*, "becomes."

[6] *zīātir*, Persian *zīādtar*, "more."

15. Khānumī la mulk i Kalhur [1] kirdia [2] tür [3]
Dinān [4] chün sadaf, qāmat chün bulür.

A lady from the Kalhur land has quarrelled,*
(Her) teeth like mother of pearl, her stature like crystal.

* i.e. quarrelled and run away from the Kalhur.

16. Khānum tuna [1] Ali, chomas,[2] tuna Dāūd
Pīchakat [3] lāwa [4] ta bünam [5] chaōwat.[6]

Lady, for Ali's sake—(thou of love) frenzied eyes—for David's sake,
Remove thy veil, that I may see thy face.

---

COUPLET 15

[1] *Kalhur*, a large district and tribe of Kurds west of Kermanshah, noted for their ferocity and power.

[2] *kirdia*, Persian *karda ast*, "has made," "done"

[3] *tür*, "quarrel." The verb here inverted is the compound *tür kirdin*, a parallel to Persian *qahr kardan*, "to quarrel," "to take offence at."

[4] *dinān*, Persian *dandān*, "teeth."

COUPLET 16.

[1] *tuna*, Persian *tur*, "for the sake of." *Tuna* also occurs in Luri and South Persian dialects.

[2] *chomas*, Persian *chashm-mast*. "frenzied."

[3] *pīchakat*, Persian *pīcha-at*, the small square black horse-hair veil worn by the women of Kermanshah and Turkish Arabia out of doors.

[4] *lāwa*, "take off," "remove," inf. *lāwān*.

[5] *bünam*, Persian *bibīnam*, "let me see."

[6] *chaōat*, Persian *chashmat*, "thy eyes."

17. **Min ki sufim sāf [1] taðba kirda bīm [2]**
**Qamar sīmā [3] dīm [4] īmān harda bīm.[5]**

I who am a Sūfī had entirely renounced (Sufism).
(When) I saw the silvery moon I was released from faith.

18. **Kāfir küshtītam [1] magar khünītam [2]**
**Kushtai khālakaī [3] chāli [4] tanītan.[5]**

Pagan, thou hast slain me, am I at feud with thee ?
Killed (am I) by the mole in the hollow of thy neck.

---

### Couplet 17.

[1] *sāf*, Persian صاف, "smooth," here used in the sense of "entirely ".

[2] *bīm*, Persian *būdam*, "I was."

[3] *sīmā*, Persian *sīmāb*, "quicksilver," "silver."

[4] *dīm*, Persian *dīdam*, Kurdish inf. *dīan*.

[5] *harda bīm*, "I was released ;" Kurdish *harda bīan*, "to be released," "to be free."

### Couplet 18.

[1] *küshtītam*, Persian *kushtī marā*, vulgar Persian *kushtīm*, "thou slewest me."

[2] *khünītam*, Persian *khūnī-at-am*, "am I at blood-feud with thee ?" *Khūnī* is the usual vulgar equivalent of *khūndārī*, "a blood-feud."

[3] *khālakaī*, Persian *khāl*, "a mole."

[4] *chāl*, "a hollow, depression," obsolescent Persian.

[5] *tanīt*, Kermanshāhī *tanī*, "the neck," the lower part of the throat.

19. **Khāli wa tū naīm [1] mar [2] wa Sekīna**
**Humā [3] kūtasaī [4] wa takht i sīna.**

A mole like thine I never saw, except on Sekīna;
She had moulded it upon the breadth of her breast.

20. Dastam bikīshīn [1] wa kur [2] giānī [3]
Wa māli [4] dūs [5] chīm [6] shaō [7] wa mīmānī.[8]

Lead me by the hand, me of little strength;
To the lover's house let us go to-night to the feast.

---

### Couplet 19.

[1] *naīm,* Persian *nadīdam,* "I saw not."

[2] *mar, magar,* "except."

[3] *humā,* Persian *ū.* The word is unusual in Kermanshāhī dialect, properly belonging to that of Sina of Kurdistān.

[4] *kūtasaī,* Persian *kūbīda ast,* "is, or has, hammered" (pounded, moulded).

### Couplet 20.

[1] *bikīshīn,* Persian *bikashīd.* Inf. *kīshin,* "to pull," "draw."

[2] *kur,* "feebleness."

[3] *giān,* Persian *jān,* "body," "soul;" *kur giānī,* "bodily weakness."

[4] *māl,* Kurdish use of the Arabic word for "house".

[5] *dūs,* Persian *dūst,* "friend," "lover."

[6] *chīm,* "let us go;" see note 5, couplet 4.

[7] *shaō,* Persian *shab,* "night."

[8] *mīmānī,* Persian *mihmānī,* "a feast," "banquet."

21. **La Sari Mīl[1] banūrī[2] Kerind diyāra[3]
Har kas dūs dirit[4] chaō intazāra.**

From Sar i Mil, by her light, Kerind is visible.
Who has a lover sits with expectant eyes.

22. La dūro[1] hātim[2] bishnāsa[3] dangam[4]
Garta[5] qarībī nīshtīa[6] la rangam.[7]

I am come from afar, hear my cry;
The dust of strange (lands) has settled upon my face.

---

COUPLET 21.

[1] *Sar-i-Mil*, the remains of an old pillar set to mark the road from Harunabad to Kerind (near Kermanshah) and distant from the latter about 5 miles.

[2] *banūrī*, Persian *bi nūrash*, "by her light."

[3] *diyāra*, "is apparent."

[4] *dirit*, Persian *dārad*, "he has."

COUPLET 22.

[1] *dūro*, Persian *dūr*, "afar."

[2] *hātim*, Persian *āmadam*, Kurdish infin. *hātin*, "to come," this form having arisen from the preservation of the older Persian verb *āīdan*, "to come," to which *h* has been prefixed, as often occurs with similar words in Kurdish.

[3] *bishnāsa*, Persian *bishinās* or *bishinū*, "hear!"

[4] *dangam*, Persian *bāngam*, "my cry."

[5] *gart*, Persian *gard*, "dust."

[6] *nīshtia*, Persian *nishasta ast*, "is sitting," "settled upon," Kurdish inf. *nīshtin*.

[7] *rangam*, "my colour," here used for "face".

23. Kamarchīn[1] i makhmal, gūshwārān wa gūsh
Mirda[2] la mazār tīārat[3] wa hūsh.

Her tunic is of velvet, earrings in her ears,
The dead from the tomb she brings to life.

24. Lāl bām[1] la zwān[2] paī[3] Lailī nāmī
Khāl dānai ferang,[4] zulf dasta i dāmī.[5]

May I be dumb of tongue, of one named Lailī
(Her) mole (is) of rare beauty, her locks a cluster of nets.

---

### Couplet 23.

[1] *kamarchīn* ; see note 5, couplet 11.

[2] *mirda*, Persian *murda*, "the dead."

[3] *tīārat*. Persian *mīārad* or *mīāvurad*, "she brings." Kurdish infinitive *āwirdin* and *hāwirdin*. This verb, together with *hātin*, takes prefixial *tī* in Kermanshāhī in the present indicative, a variant of the similarly used *di* and *da* in more northern dialects.

### Couplet 24.

[1] *bām*, Persian *bāsham*, "may I be."

[2] *zwān*, Persian *zabān*, "tongue."

[3] *pai*, Persian *barāyi*, "for."

[4] *dānai ferang*, a term used in Kurdish to express any small article of great beauty.

[5] *dasta i dāmī*, a cluster of nets (for the ensnaring of the enamoured), a common Persian metaphor.

25. Banā kird ghārat i sarmāya i hūsham
Lungi Majnūnī aō dā [1] wa dusham.

She undertook the plunder of my stock of sense,
The cloth of Majnūn she gave me for my back.*

* i.e. she made me like Majnūn, mad for love of Lailī.

26. Chan [1] jaur chan jefā, chan khākisāri
Shwān [2] i bi muz [3] u haqq nā diyārī.

How much trouble, how much anguish, how much lamenting?
Nights without reward, and right unrecognised!

27. Sa jwōām ka [1] ta dil niā [2] būm [3]
Kam das [4] la dāmām Shaikh o mulla būm.

Then release me that my heart be at rest,
That my hand be not stretched out to skirts of Mulla and Shaikh!

---

COUPLET 25.

[1] *dā*, Persian *dād*, "gave."

COUPLET 26.

[1] *chan*, Persian *chand*, used in Kurdish indifferently for "how much" and "how many".
[2] *shwān*, Persian *shabān*, "nights." This plural for *shab* is obsolete in Persian.
[3] *muz*, Persian *muzd*, "reward," "price."

COUPLET 27.

[1] *sa jwōam ka*, Persian *pas javābam kun* "then make me my reply," i.e. "release me".
[2] *dil niā*, "with heart at rest."
[3] *būm*, Persian *bishavam*, "that I become."
[4] *das*, Persian *dast*, "hard."

28. Fedāī mālakai [1] pāyi Paraōit [2] bām [3]
Fedai dīdakai [4] shaō bī khaōit [5] bām.

May I be the sacrifice of thy house at Paraō's foot,
Sacrifice of thy eyes upon sleepless nights.

29. Har [1] tīaīt [2] har chīt [3] cham [4] wa gilāwa [5]
Chün kaok [6] i nisār khīāl wa hilāwa.[7]

(Thou) ever coming, ever going, with straining eyes,
Like a partridge of the desert rising to fly.

---

COUPLET 28.

[1] *mālakai,* "a house," the termination *-akai* being quite optional and ruled by no custom.

[2] *Paraōit,* "thy, Paraō," the possessive referring to *mālakai* in conformity with Persian usage, when a possessive is added to the last of a series of nouns used adjectivally. Paraō is a high range of mountains north-west of Kermanshah.

[3] *bām,* Persian *bāsham,* "may I be." See note 1, couplet 24.

[4] *dīdakai,* Persian *dīda,* "eyes."

[5] *khaōit,* "thy, sleep," the possessive qualifying *dīdakai.*

COUPLET 29.

[1] *har,* the same word as in Persian, but possessing in Kurdish a wider meaning, here signifying "incessantly".

[2] *tīaīt,* Persian *mīāyī.* See note 3, couplet 23.

[3] *chīt,* Persian *mīravī,* "thou goest."

[4] *cham,* Persian *chashm,* "eyes."

[5] *gilāwa,* "tiredness, straining." The word is *gilā* with termination *-awa* or *-wa,* which is frequently added in Kurdish poetry.

[6] *kaōk,* Persian *kabk,* "partridge."

[7] *hilāwa,* "flying," "rising."

30 Chaōm kaft[1] wa zīd u māwān[2] i Lailī
Anūm[3] jüsh hāwird,[4] gīriyām[5] khailī.

My eyes fell upon the place of Lailī;
My grief came to boiling, and my tears many.

31. Min ki Kerind shār[1] dīm[2] wa wīrāna[3]
Sar i Pul[4] dīm wa jāy bāyaqush[5] khāna.

I (who) have seen Kerind town a ruin,
And Sar i Pul the place of owls' nesting.

The word *ki* is here not necessarily to be translated as a relative pronoun, being used in an emphatic sense, which is a common use in vulgar Persian as in Kurdish, as Persian *man ki chand martaba guftam?* "how many times have I spoken?"

---

COUPLET 30.

[1] *kaft*, Persian *uftād*, "fell," from Kurdish inf. *kaftin*, "to fall."
[2] *zīd u māwān*, a Kurdish expression somewhat equivalent to the Persian *maqām va makān*, "residence and place."
[3] *anūm*, Persian *andūh-am*, "my grief."
[4] *hāwird*, Persian *āvard*, "brought."
[5] *gīriyā*, Persian *giriā*, "tears."

COUPLET 31.

[1] *shār*, Persian *shahr*, "a town."
[2] *dīm*, Persian *dīdam*, "I saw."
[3] *wīrāna*, Persian *vīrān*, "ruin," a now obsolete word.
[4] *Sar i Pul*, or more correctly Sar i Pul i Zohāb, near the Perso-Turkish frontier post of Qasr i Shirin, a Kurdish town.
[5] *bāyaqush*, "an owl" (Turkish).